LOVE

and

LOSS

A Virginia Girl's

Civil War Diary

1863–1868

by

Mary Octavia Smith Tabb

Paxton Press

Hampton, Virginia

Mary Octavia's actual diary

LOVE

and

LOSS

A Virginia Girl's Civil War Diary

1863–1868

by

Mary Octavia Smith Tabb

Smithville, York County, Virginia

*"I hav(e) no Confidante into whose ears to breath(e)
my feelings with the exception of this little book...."*
Tavey Smith, September 20, 1863

Paxton Press

HAMPTON

For Mary Elizabeth Hambleton and Jean Clarke

Cover and Design
Marshall Rouse McClure

ISBN 978-0-578-04559-7

Paxton Press
Hampton, Virginia

CONTENTS

ILLUSTRATIONS

Mary Octavia "Tavey" Smith Tabb (1845–1924)

Picture taken from family group photograph (below), from the album of her granddaughter, Virginia "Genia" Tabb Thomas (1910–2005).

Aunt Ressie, Geo. L., Grandma Tavey, Mrs. Asher

"Aunt Ressie" was Theresa Smith (1848–1924), sister-in-law to Tavey and wife of Levin S. Smith. "Geo. L." was George Levin Smith, Jr. (1909–1999), grandson of Levin S. Smith. "Mrs. Asher" was maternal grandmother of George Levin Smith, Jr., and "Aunt Ressie's" mother.

FOREWORD

This diary by Mary Octavia Smith Tabb was started during the Civil War beginning in January 1863 and ending October 1868.

She was the grandmother of Mary Elizabeth Tabb Hambleton and Jean Cary Tabb Forrest Clarke. Mary, who lives in Norman, Oklahoma, was married to Edgar A. Hambleton, a retired Air Force colonel, now deceased. They met in Tabb, Virginia, while Colonel Hambleton was still on active duty at nearby Langley Air Force Base. Jean, who is twice widowed, was first married to William Samuel Forrest, a Virginia waterman, and then to B. T. Clarke, a retired Methodist minister. She currently lives on the York River in Gloucester, Virginia.

The home where Mary Octavia presumably lived while writing this diary was the one where she was born. Still standing in York County, Virginia, it has been in the Smith family for over 300 years. Although the home has undergone numerous modifications over the years, the original building remains as a part of the present structure. At the time Mary Octavia kept her diary, the area or settlement was known as Smithville, so named for her family.

Mary Octavia was seventeen years old in 1863 when she started her diary. In 1871, she married Alexander C. Tabb who died at the age of 32. In 1893, Mary Octavia was chartered as postmistress of Smithville, and maintained the post office in her home where she sold stamps and handled other postal requirements of area residents. Later, the community was renamed Tabb and was an active post office serving a large community until the 1980s, at which time it became part of the Yorktown, Virginia postal system.

Mary Octavia's writing reveals the heart of a young woman who has encountered heartache at a very young age and in troubling times. She is poetic in her use of words and expresses herself in a voice that can resonate with others in North or South, in her time or in our time. We appreciate the willingness of Mary Octavia's granddaughters to share this very personal writing with us.

L. Roane Hunt, Historian, Gloucester, Virginia

PREFACE

A good diary can be a well of hidden treasures to provide a glimpse into the past. Not only is a diary a personal repository of the writer's most private thoughts, but it might also be an almanac of the time in which the writer of the diary lived.

Tavey Smith was a teenager at the time of the Civil War. Living in rural southeastern Virginia, she was peripherally involved with the war itself and, especially, one of its victims. She, also a victim, found herself in a sisterhood of thousands of women in the South – and North, too – who had to reinvent themselves in order to survive. Their resolve to assume the role of father to children, as well as mother; manager of businesses left leaderless; plantation overseers and farmers; and, sometimes, even soldiers, was seen in communities all over the country, especially the South. Small wonder such Southern women became known as "steel magnolias."

Tavey's diary is printed *exactly as she wrote it.* She reveals her sensitivities, her emotional states and her activities with directness and honesty. She does not seem embarrassed to be writing about her frustrations and concerns. Perhaps she never considered the possibility that others would be reading what she was thinking and feeling.

The diary also shows the daily busyness that Tavey endured. A separate selection of bits of information gleaned from her diary reveals a glimpse into Tavey's everyday activities at work and at ease. Thus, the complete diary gives an objective, as well as subjective, view of a young girl approaching womanhood in Civil War Virginia.

Tavey, a Southern sympathizer, was a dutiful daughter, a hard worker, and an accomplished young woman who was interested in what lay in the world beyond her home in the small community of Smithville. She was kind and thoughtful and considerate of others, most of the time. She knew right from wrong. Her uncertainty in her relationships with others is almost universal, as is the sad longing and sorrowful regret that she experiences. She can relate to almost any person who has lost a loved one.

Billie Paxton Einselen, Hampton, Virginia

INTRODUCTION

This diary by Mary Octavia Smith Tabb was started during the Civil War beginning in January 1863 and ending October 1868. She wrote about teaching school for local children and assisting in the family enterprise of providing lodging for travelers and meals for the community. She wrote about a special young man of her favor who died early in the war that took place nearby. She lamented greatly his death and noted its anniversary with regrets. In 1871, Mary Octavia Smith married Alexander Tabb, who died six years later at the age of 32. Many of the soldiers who survived the war died young. She did not remarry in the remaining forty-seven years of her life.

At the time of Mary Octavia's diary, the area or settlement was known as Smithville. The Smiths and Tabbs were related by marriage. Mary Octavia was seventeen years old in 1863 when she started her diary. Later, in 1893, she was chartered as postmistress of Smithville and maintained the post office in her home. Here she sold stamps and handled other postal requirements of the local residents. Later, the area was renamed Tabb and remained an active post office serving a large community until the 1980s, at which time it became part of the Yorktown postal services.

Mary Elizabeth Tabb Hambleton and Jean Clarke,
the granddaughters of Mary Octavia

ACKNOWLEDGMENTS

My sister and I are blessed that we have come to know better our Grandmother Tavey through her diary. Our sharing it with others has been the result of the labor of friends whom we must acknowledge:

To Tavey, first of all, we owe gratitude for her penning her thoughts over those long-ago years.

Phyllis and Roane Hunt, our friends, have given endless help and encouragement, as well as meticulous research into the family history. We could not have undertaken this project without Roane's infinite patience in copying the diary's transcription to disk.

Dorothy Rouse-Bottom, a scholar of history in Hampton, began the production process of putting the diary in print.

Theresa M. Hammond, Librarian of the William E. Rouse Library in Hampton, suggested historical material and researched relevant pieces of information.

Michael Cobb, Curator of the Hampton History Museum and a Civil War enthusiast, answered numerous questions about living conditions and life in Tidewater Virginia at the time of the Civil War.

Daniel William Forrest, my son, made suggestions and provided photos. While his son-in-law, Chris Rollins, drove a truck, he also assisted in the rescue of his son (my grandson), Daniel William Forrest II, and me from a mud hole on a rainy Thanksgiving afternoon as we sought and found Tavey's grave in a country cemetery. Danny II now lives in Tavey's house with his wife, Kate, and their two daughters.

Robert Carol Emerson, a retired minister with a lifelong interest in local history, gave valuable information about the family and area. He also provided the inscription on Tavey's tombstone.

Billie Paxton Einselen, a self-described "words-person" in Hampton, added historical information to better glimpse the life of Tavey. Most importantly, she continued and completed the production process of the diary before printing.

Marshall Rouse McClure of Norfolk designed the diary and the cover. We think Tavey would approve and applaud.

And to my dear sister, Mary Elizabeth, who painstakingly transcribed Tavey's diary, I am forever grateful, as are other members of the family and friends.

Jean Tabb Forrest Clarke
Gloucester, Virginia

TAVEY: BEFORE THE DIARY

Mary Octavia Smith, Tavey (with a long A) begins her diary the first day of 1863 when she was seventeen years old. This was some eighteen months after the Battle of Big Bethel, which took place on June 10, 1861, near her York County home in southeastern Virginia. Big Bethel, one of the earliest land battles of the Civil War, provided the opportunity for Union forces, which held Fort Monroe at the foot of the Chesapeake Bay in Hampton, to test local Confederate forces as part of their blockade of the Bay. The out-of-the-area Federal troops, disorganized and repulsed, retreated to Hampton, about ten miles away, and Newport News, a bit farther. Although inconclusive, Big Bethel was considered a Confederate victory. Hamptonians, who were mainly Southern sympathizers, burned their town on August 7, 1861, rather than have Federal troops occupy their homes and businesses.

Tavey was born on March 18, 1845, to Mary Anne Howard Smith and George W. Smith in York County in southeastern Virginia. The home was in the community called "Smithville" on the Old Stage Road between Yorktown and Hampton. Tavey's grandfather, Levin Smith, had come to York County from Accomack County on Virginia's Eastern Shore.

We know that Tavey had siblings: Sarah Frances, two years older; Levin, two years younger; George, six years younger; and Margaret Lee ("Maggie"), the baby who was sixteen years younger. Tavey mentions them throughout the diary.

Tavey was an accomplished reader and writer. She was an exception, as in 1863 not every woman in the United States was literate. Living in a rural area, she lacked someone with whom she could share her thoughts, ideas, and feelings, especially those feelings of grief. Thus her diary becomes an outlet to whom she bares her heart and her soul. She has lost a great love at a young age, for whom she grieves for far too long. As she had no one with whom she could express her grief, the reader, thus, becomes her listener.

Monday, Sept 20th, 1863

"O how sad and lonely I sometimes feel, yes, unhappy. Little doth the passerby know how or why one over whose head only 18 summers have passed so swiftly with its joys and sorrows should thus complain... I, having no Confidante into whose ears to breath(e) my feelings with the exception of this little book, and it is not often I pen them here...."

Billie Einselen
Hampton, Virginia

DIARY ENTRIES OF
MARY OCTAVIA SMITH TABB
(1845–1924)

TRANSCRIBED FROM THE DIARY OF
MARY OCTAVIA SMITH TABB, OUR GRANDMOTHER AND
MOTHER OF OUR FATHER, HOWARD TABB.

1863 January 1st — The New Years day has past and now it is night, such a lovely day it has been. Would that the state of affairs were in accordance with the day, but alas it cannot be. As I look back to the past year how gloomy a greater part of it seems, and oh, it is too true that the many dear forms and faces I have known, some of them are no more. Ah, how sad to reflect on, to know that cherished hopes and bright antici- pations lie withering dying under the scorching effects of Civil commotion caused by the blind fanaticism of an invading foe who threatens all that the heart of our Nation holds dear. I have heard today of a successful raid made by Gen. Stuart on the north side of the Rappahannock. May Victory continue still to gleam upon us, and each day may I have some glorious achievement to record, performed by the gallantry of our Southern Sons. How many cherished ones have fallen in this strife and many hearts have been robbed of its **PRIDE**, its **HOPE**, its **ALL** and now remains cheerless. This morning sister Maggie and myself walked to see Louisa Turner, she is confined to her bed, but I hope ere long she will be restored to health. We carried her a letter from her Brother, how glad she was to receive it, has been so long since she had heard from him. I must now close, as I have some work to do. I hope my journal will grow more cheerful as the days pass along.

Friday, January 2 — Another one of those bright days. Nature seems to be rejoicing in her loveliness. Still the heart seems void in every pleasure that gladdened it in the past. When I turn to that picture the ("past") how joyous are some of the scenes pictured there, it seems as if wandering to some far off dream—land, where there arise forms, and faces, of dear ones that have gladdened our path in life's bright day. And to know that those dear forms have vanished with the stream of time, how sad is the thought. My heart has known and felt the effects caused by the unyielding hand of fate, yet still I bend in meek submission to **HIM**, "Who doeth all things well." Perhaps it was not meant that I should have set my heart so much on earthly things but still the human heart is too weak to see its many errors. And such was my case, too happy to last. Mrs. M Cook, Lizzie, Victoria and Mrs. King were to see us this evening. Mrs. King and V. remained until after supper. Mrs. C and Lizzie left before. I hope soon to hear some news.

Saturday, January 3rd — The days still continue mild and pretty but I do not think it will last long as the atmosphere seems damp. Lizzie walked over this afternoon and staid (*sp*) until after supper. She would insist on my going home with her. I went and staid about an hour, the moon shines very brightly and but for the cold it would have been a pleasant walk. Ah! How much I should like to know if our dear Soldiers are enjoying the luxury of a large fire this cool damp night. I sincerely hope they are comfortable as their limited means of a soldier will allow, for it is a hard life at best. I hope some friendly hand will give them food, and shelter as much as possible. But there is One eye that never sleeps, who will watch over them, in every time of need. Guide them safely Father through these dark clouds of civil warfare. I must now prepare for bed.

Sunday, January 4th — The Holy Sabbath day has passed without any unusual occurrence to mar its quietude. Oh, that peace could have dawned with it and friends and relatives could have assembled in their respective places of worship to offer up praises to their God. Ah how many have met at a Throne of Grace will never more be permitted to assemble again on earth but joyful will be the day when they shall meet in their Heavenly Home, where the cold and blighting hand of fate can never chill their joys. I was greeted with a pleasant surprise caused by receiving a letter from my Cousin H. How glad I was to hear from him, his letter was quite interesting. I shall answer it soon and hope ere long I shall receive another. Sister and myself walked this evening to see Lizzie and remained until after supper. Mrs Wornam was there. Mother went to Aunt Mollie's. They are all well.

Monday, January 5th — Today like its predecessors has been mild and beautiful. Mother went to Mrs. Cooke's this afternoon and remained until after tea. Victoria came this evening and intends spending the night with us. I am glad to see her and hope she may spend her time agreeably. How many sad reflections my heart can sum up in a few moments this afternoon. Sister went to walk with Mother and while left to my own reflections quietly did my thoughts wander back to the past and with it came a form of a friend who is no more, it makes me so sad to know such is true. I am almost ready to sometimes exclaim "Why is it thus?" Victoria seems so lively I wonder if she ever feels as depressed as my own heart sometimes is. Surely she cannot or her laugh would not ring out so merry, but the laughing face is not always an index to the heart, for I know that by experience. I hope tomorrow will be clear, as Aunt Mollie is coming.

Tuesday, January 6th — This morning the sky was unclouded which seemed to foretell a pleasant day but soon after breakfast the air was damp and cool which rendered the day quite unpleasant. Levin brought Aunt Mollie and Cousin Anna here, they spent the day with us. It seemed very strange to see dear Aunt Mollie here again, I was delighted to see them. This after noon was dull and rainy. I sigh to know that with the past has vanished so many joys that seemed destined to decay. A sad foreboding still around me linger but oh, there are reasons for it which are useless to dwell upon.

Wednesday, January 7th — The dark clouds that obscured the brightness of yesterday vanished last night. I arose this morning I found a beautiful bright sky. Cousin Sarah and Aunt Rebecca spent the day with us today which made it pass swiftly away. The weather is quite cold. I should like to know how our brave boys are fareing this cold night. I hope they will not suffer for the want of fire and clothes but I am afraid they will. May that eye that never sleeps look pityingly upon. I must read and prepare for bed. Victoria went home this morning.

Thursday, January 8th — The day has been dark and cold, colder than yesterday. This afternoon Victoria came and brought me a letter from Cousin Howard. It has been a long time coming, poor fellow, he seems so much distressed about his Father. Shortly after Victoria left, Mrs. Crandol, Rebecca, Jennie and Emily came to walk with Sallie McIntosh who is here with us tonight. I am very glad to see her. I forgot to mention that Miss Moore and Mr. McIntosh, they came also but did not stay long. The Yankee steamer Monitor has gone to the bottom of the ocean, she sprung a leak and went down on the 31st of December, 1862 so the pride and boast of the Yankee navy is no more. Thank God for it for to Him is all praise due. It is reported with the Yankees that Vicksburg and Murfreesboro have been captured by them but I hope it is false. Sallie taught me to make rose tatting tonight. I must now stop.

Friday, Jan 9th — When I awoke this morning the ground was covered with snow. The trees looked very beautiful covered with the drapering of winter. It remained cloudy all the morning but the afternoon was beautiful. Mr. McIntosh came for Sallie this evening. I was sorry she should go but we could not prevail on her to stay any longer. We received a paper today and the Yankees claim a great victory at Murfreesboro, Tenn. but I hope it is false. Gen. Rains is reported killed, also another of our Generals. Such a pity it is that any of our heroes should have to fall. If it is true, how unhappy are the feelings of their family and friends for the fate of their brave companions. I sympathize with them in their bereavement although I don't know them.

Saturday, Jan 10th — Dark clouds have eclipsed the brightness of last afternoon, and it has been a dark cloudy day and this evening the rain poured in torrents. In thinking of bygone hours, it depresses my spirits. I never wander to those scenes which fond memory recalls without feelings of sadness. It seems as if I have awoke from some sweet dream to the stern reality and with my wakeing I sigh to know that some who blessed those dreams are with the departed. It is such a reflection that is painful to dwell upon. The Yankees have been foiled in their attempts to capture Vicksburg. How glad I am to know it has not fallen to the hands of a merciless foe, God grant that it never may. My trusting heart shall offer up praises and thanks to that Kind Father who has so mercifully supported us through this trying ordeal. Would that this strife would cease crowned with glory for the Southern cause.

Sunday, Jan 11th — The day has been cool but not very clear. Mother, Par and Maggie spent the day at Uncle Frank's. Sister, Levin, Georgie and myself remained at home. We spent a quiet day well befitting the holy day that has been so quiet. No one has been here today but Mrs. Cooke's servant (Caroline) who came to bring us some socks. I feel so depressed at times, I seem to live over the past, as I glance at my own heart how many buried memories lie strewn here and there, memories that are dearly cherished. It is surely a hard task to forget, still I do not wish entirely erased as they bring before my imagination some sweet memorial of bygone hours that have fled. Alas, too swiftly. Sallie, Miss Moore and Victoria came by this morn.

Monday, Jan 12th — The bright sun gleamed forth today casting his light upon surrounding objects. It has been such a sweet day so mild and bright. Mr. Hopkins took dinner with us. I have heard no news of any importance. I hope I have some bright victory to record before many days. Why does the sigh escape so heavily from my heart? Although "my face still wears its wonty (sp) glee." Yet that dark Image sadness still lives within my heart and how little does the observer know the many feelings too deep for utterance that are its constant inmates. When I come to read those feelings deeply, it is with reluctance to know its fondest hopes have fled. I practiced a short while this morning. I must now retire as it is late. Today a year ago how different we were there surrounded by our southern friends and what a happy day I spent. It was Sunday, I had the pleasure of enjoying the company of two highly prized friends.

Tuesday, January 13th — Today has been similar to yesterday with the exception of the latter part of the afternoon when the sky became somewhat cloudy and tonight it is quite dark and cloudy. It is truly wonderful that the mind can wander back and almost live the past over again in a few short moments, but it is with regret when I compare the past with the present. There is so much disparity between the two, the first so happy, now so unhappy. Yet I must not murmur "Not my will but thine O Lord be done." I must now prepare for bed where I hope to be blessed with pleasant dreams.

Wednesday, Jan 14th — A vast difference exist between the 14th of Jan. 1862 and the 14th of Jan. 1863. Tonight a year ago, how buoyant was every feeling that surrounded my heart, its pulsations were those of gaiety. I was at a party and was enjoying myself so much, the tide of hope, sweet hope was gushing warm and strong. It was not disturbed by fears of the future but it glided tranquilly on, the star of Hope was gleaming brightly like a sweet beacon to lure us on as the Past has unmasked. Hearts were light and cheeks were flushed with glow. It has been almost like spring today. Aunt Sarah, Laura, Ida and little Sallie spent the day with us. I have heard today our gallant Magruder has whipped the Yankees, in Texas, and has captured several of their gunboats among them the Harriet Lane.

Thursday, Jan 15th — It has looked and felt like spring all day but it clouded up this afternoon. The wind is blowing quite hard. I expect by morning the weather will be cool, the sky is clear and the little myriads of stars are peering brightly from their heavenly homes. We received a newspaper tonight and it seems like our future is nearing a glorious issue for our cause. Surely our Heavenly Father in his benificent mercy has led us safely on. May He continue to smile upon our every effort and at last grant us peace and Independence. We have recaptured Galveston and taken several vessels. How thankful I am for it. We should all with an humble trusting heart offer up praise to Him who has given us the Victory.

Friday, Jan 16th — A dull rainy morning, the wind has been blowing quite hard, it is very cold tonight. I deeply feel for our dear boys who are exposed to this cold piercing wind, how they must suffer if they are not comfortably clad, but I hope ere this everything needful as far as possible has been contributed for their comfort. My heart yearns to behold again the faces of those dear friends, but it cannot be for they must (be) away to duty and drive the invader from this precious soil which they so long polluted. I must now prepare for retiring.

Saturday, Jan 17th — The sun rose brightly this morn from an unclouded sky, the day has been most beautiful but very cold, the ground is frozen hard. We received a paper today, the contents which were quite interesting. We have captured Holly Springs, Miss. and a great deal of government property, and our heroic boys have bravely and successfully defended our glorious Vicksburg. May they with an unshaken confidence in Him who rules above continue to hurl back all the forces that the boasting invader can bring against them.

Sunday, Jan 18th — It has been very cold all day. Sister and myself walked over to see Lizzie this afternoon. Eddie and Lizzie came home with us but did not remain long. There is no news of any importance.

Monday, Jan 19th — Has been a cold but lovely day. The earth seems so fair, yet the heart is sad, sad. Ah, how long is this to last, will the silvery lineing of this dark cloud ever, be revealed to those who anxiously awaited its appearance. I trust to our Heavenly Father it may soon appear. We received a *Southern Almanac* tonight.

Tuesday, Jan 20th — A dull dark day, it commenced raining this afternoon and it still continues. Just as we arose from the supper table, some one knocked loudly at the door and on asking who they were, they replied, a Union friend. As we are not in the habit of receiving those unwelcome visitors, we would not open the door. After asking various questions, we called Jack who brought them in. They proved to be two Yankee officers. They are going to remain all night. The war question was brought up and Sister and myself were tested strongly for the Southern side. We brought before our recent victories. We

talked secession so strongly that they knew not what to say. I
was determined to hold up for my rights and expressed myself
very freely. The wind is blowing very hard. I trust the Lord
may be with our brave boys and lead them on to Victory.

Wednesday, Jan 21st — It has been cloudy and cool. Lizzie came
over this morning and after dinner we walked to Uncle Kit
Curtis's. We had a wet walk, we lost our way on returning.
Uncle Kit came with us nearly home. Lizzie is with us tonight.

Thursday, Jan 22d — Another of those cold dark days, it is now
raining quite hard. Par went to Hampton today, he brought
back a paper but there wasn't much news of any importance. I
hope our Soldiers are well provided with tents, if not I know
they must suffer with cold exposed to this cold rain. Oh, the
horrors of war, how distressing, if it is so horrible to me,
much more so it must be to those who are exposed to its stern
reality.

Friday, Jan 23d — Still cloudy and cold. Nothing of interest has
transpired today. Several gentlemen were here this afternoon.

Saturday, Jan 24th — The weather still cloudy. Sister and myself
walked to Mrs. Crandol's this afternoon but did not find her
home. All the girls were at home. Eddie was there and came
with us, and staid here until after ten o'clock. Mr. Hudgins was
here this evening, also Lizzie came over this morning but left
before dinner. We received a paper today, but there is not any
news very important.

Sunday, Jan 25th — It has been clearer today than yesterday, and
this afternoon the Sun made his appearance. Me, my thoughts
sometimes almost amount to despair.

Monday, Jan 26th — It seems as if we are not going to have any
good weather for some time as it still continues cloudy. How I
wish it would clear away, as dark days are so gloomy which
depresses our system also. Mother and Myself spent the afternoon at Mrs. Cook's. Lizzie came home with us, and is going
to remain all night with us. I am glad of her company. I have
rolled her hair up tonight and I expect in the morning she will
be curly headed Lizzie.

Tuesday, Jan 27th — A rainy day, it seems as if its going to rain all the week. Lizzie left this morning after breakfast. She left soon as she expected company. I wrote a letter to Jenny Dear, this morning. I hope ere long I will get an answer. How delighted I should be to receive a letter from her friendly hand, it would somewhat revive my drooping spirits. Will there never come a time when peace sweet peace shall resume her sway. Would that it would hasten to the hearts that are anxiously waiting its advent.

Wednesday, Jan 28th — The weather still inclement. A Yankee Captain came here today and brought a paper, in which I see an account where Burnside set out to cross the Rappahannock, but was obliged to return to his old camp ground on account of the storm and I expect for want of courage also. How thankful I am that his plan was a failure. I hope it may be his fate to meet with reverses. Eddie was here this afternoon and told our fortunes. He did not leave until 9 o'clock this evening.

Thursday, Jan 29th — It commenced to snow this morning soon, but did not last long, the clouds soon cleared away and the weather today has been clear. We have not heard any news today, but I hope when we do it will prove good for us.

Friday, Jan 30th — A clear bright day. Lizzie came here this morning. Jennie and Rebecca Crandol were here this afternoon, they came by Mrs. Cook's and Lizzie came with them. Jennie and Rebecca left after supper. Lizzie remained with us and will stay till morning. Eddie and Kit came over this evening and we practiced our charade.

Saturday, Jan 31st — Has been a lovely day. Kit and Eddie came here this morning and we practiced our charade so as to be able to perform it this evening. We had Mrs. and Mr. Cooke, Mr. Hudgins, Jennie, Rebecca and Martha Crandol to see us perform, it was conducted very nicely. I took the part of Mrs. Lockett, Lizzie as Ada Lockett, Mrs. L's daughter, Sister as Susan the servant girl, Eddie as Mr. Sparks, and Kit as Beauchamps. All seemed to enjoy themselves. I hear from a Yankee paper today that the Alabama has sunk an ironclad. I hope by the Help of a beneficient Providence we will continue to triumph. Would that those dear boys who are far away could have been with us tonight to witness our charade.

Sunday, Feb 1st — Today has been somewhat cloudy. We received a newspaper and the Confederate Ship *Florida* has destroyed four vessels. Sister and myself went to see Louisa this afternoon. Mother went to Mrs. Cooke's and Eddie and Lizzie came with her but returned about dark.

Monday, Feb 2d — A clear day. I practiced nearly an hour this morning. Sister and myself spent the afternoon at Mrs. Cooke's. The Yankees have sent a formidable force against Vicksburg. I hope, by the help of our Heavenly Father, we may again drive them back. I hear today that we have gained a victory at Blackwater, Va. How thankful I am for it.

Tuesday, Feb 3d — When I awoke this morning the ground was covered with snow. It continued to snow until about ten A.M. and tonight it is quite beautiful.

Wednesday, Feb 4th — Was a clear bright day but did not melt the snow much. Ah, I should like to know how our dear boys fared such cold weather.

Thursday, Feb 5th — It clouded up thick last night and this morning it snowed quite fast until nearly ten o'clock. It then commenced to rain and it has been pouring almost incessantly. Ah, sad change has indeed come over my heart which is known to me alone. True I am not always sad for I do not have always time to reflect but when I do those reflections are sad yet sweet.

Friday, Feb 6th — A dull rainy day, there is not any news of any importance.

Saturday, Feb 7th — A bright clear day, there is not any news of importance. I hope to get a paper soon.

Sunday, Feb 8th — Today has been cool but not very clear. Louisa and Julia came to see us this afternoon. Cousin Nancy Wade came also.

Monday, Feb 9th — A clear bright day. I practiced this morning about an hour and a half. Gen. Magruder is still active in Texas, he has captured Sabine Pass, may he continue to prosper in our cause. Lizzie came here this afternoon and is going to remain with us all night.

Tuesday, Feb 10th — Has been like spring all day. Lizzie went home this morning and came back this afternoon and Sister, Lizzie and myself went to Mrs. Crandol's and Mrs. King's. Eddie went and came with us. He went to the store tonight to get a paper, and when he came back some one halted him, and it proved to be several Yankees whom under pretense of orders came in and searched the house from bottom to top, not even excepting our chambers. How long are things to remain thus. Will there never, never come a day of retribution? My heart pines for its advent, surely these things will not always be for there is ONE who will avenge our wrongs. It is that for which many a brave man are now struggling. Yes! and they will redress them or die in the attempt.

Wednesday, Feb 11th — A cloudy day with a little rain. There is not any news.

Thursday, Feb 12th — This morning was a very dense fog but it disappeared about twelve o'clock and still remained cloudy. Lizzie came over this afternoon, and remained until after supper. Sister went home with Lizzie and I am alone in my room tonight. I must now prepare for bed where I hope to be blessed with pleasant dreams.

Friday, Feb 13th — A bright mild day. Sister returned home this morning. Victoria and Mrs. King were over to see us this morning. Lizzie is with me tonight.

Saturday, Feb 14th — How bright and beautiful is all nature. Yes, all things that God has created seem contented except man, whose heart is so vile. How sad to think that the noblest being formed by the Creator is rendering itself obnoxious from exorcising their angry passions upon each other and those passions springing from that bitter germ, envy, which is the destroyer of all human bliss. It seems as if our enemies are so dead to justice that search out every way to wreak their wrath against us. It is now reported that Norfolk is burnt, sad, sad is it if so that the invader should enter, spoil and burn our cities to appease their desire for vengeance. I truly sympathise with its inhabitants whose sufferings must be almost unbearable. What feelings must fill their heart to see their firesides around which are clustered so many hallowed memories desecrated and they wandering, seeking for refuge from the chilly winter winds. Ah, but is there not One with whom they can hold sweet communion, who will comfort them in their afflictions and Who has said. "Vengeance is mine, I will repay." How consoling it is to the sorrowing heart to know there is one who will avenge our wrongs.

Sunday, Feb 15th — The Holy Sabbath day has passed silently away. The weather has been cloudy accompanied by a shower of rain this afternoon. It seems as if this unholy strife is wearing away our very existence. Oh, for peace once more to resume her gentle sway. When it does come, perhaps we will better appreciate the blessings favoured us by a kind Providence.

Monday, Feb 16th — Has been cloudy, the sun shining at intervals. Victoria and Granville were here this afternoon but left before tea.

Tuesday, Feb 17th — An incessant rain from early in the morning and it still continues making me feel lonesome yet relapsing into thoughtful mood, as it comes pattering upon the pane.

Wednesday, Feb 18th — It is still raining. Sister and myself received an invitation today to attend the marriage of Miss Phillips and Mr. Crandol which is to take place tomorrow afternoon at three o'clock. My friendly wish is that she may be happy in the new change which is about to be made in her life. Sister and myself will not attend. My feelings do not at all corrolate with the pleasures which are normally predominant on such occasions.

Thursday, Feb 19th — A dull dark day. Miss Phillips and Mr. Crandol were married this afternoon. Mr. Cooke went to the wedding and came by tonight. Mr. Hudgins has gotten home after having been retained at Old Point as a prisoner for nearly a week. We received a paper this evening. The Emperor Napoleon has offered his mediation to the Lincoln government and should they respect it, it is said a speedy recognition of the South will soon follow.

Friday, Feb 20th — A clear day, we received a paper but there is not any news of importance.

Saturday, Feb 21st — Clear and bright in the morning but clouded up late in the afternoon, one guest came today.

Sunday, Feb 22d — The anniversary of our illustrous Washington's birthday. It is snowing and hailing and the ground is covered over with snow. The Alabama has again captured three of the enemy's brigs. Ah, would that this strife would cease, thankful I am that our Heavenly Father still smiles upon us.

Monday, Feb 23d — Cloudy in the first part of the morning but cleared away towards noon.

Tuesday, Feb 24th — Clear and cold, no news of any importance. Ah, how desolate seems the once joyous feelings that gladdened my heart. As the Poet remarks "Friends have been scattered." It is too true that such is really so.

Wednesday, Feb 25th — Still continues clear. We received paper today, but there is not any news of importance.

Thursday, Feb 26th — The weather has been changeable, sometimes cloudy and then again the sun shining. I wrote a letter to Mollie Curtis. Mrs. Crandol is going to Norfolk tomorrow if nothing happens to prevent and will carry my letter.

Friday, Feb 27th — Still continues cloudy. There is not any news of interest. The Yankee gunboats *Queen of the West* and *Indianaiola* have not been heard from.

Saturday, Feb 28th — A dull cloudy morning. While we were sitting at our work this morning greatly to our surprise we saw Aunt Rebecca and Cousin Sarah coming. They walked all the way from home. We were delighted to see them. They are going to remain all night, Winter is about to leave us, and as we look back, how sad are some of the changes wrought since this time last year. Then kind, true friends were here to bless and protect but alas, alas, those golden hours have flown. It has been raining quite fast this afternoon.

Sunday, March 1st — Spring has stolen almost imperceptible upon us, the Winter has gone, many a spring flower will bloom sweetly o'er the graves of the weary soldier whose toil and warfare is over and have gone I hope to reside with the pure in heart. Full many a sweet violet will rear its modest head, above his mound, and seems in its sweet innocence to say, sleep on, dear one, you are not forgotten. Cousin Sarah left for home this afternoon, Aunt Rebecca remained as she was much indisposed. It has cleared away and the sun shone very brightly this afternoon.

Monday, March 2d — The Sun shone mild and lovely. Aunt Rebecca and Mother went to see Cousin Elvie this morning. Patsy carried them, and brought me some flowers for planting in my garden. Lizzie, Kit and Eddie were here this afternoon, we acted two charades for Aunt Rebecca, Contest and Phantom. Lizzie returned home about 10 o'clock P.M. We received a newspaper tonight. We have captured the Queen of the West and our little Vicksburg still frowns furiously upon her besiegers.

Tuesday, March 3d — The Sun shone very bright this morning, the sky a little cloudy this afternoon. Mother, Aunt Rebecca and myself walked over to Uncle Kit's this afternoon, we had a fine time battling over the briers and bushes. We received a paper today. There is not much news, except some from Western Va. where our forces killed and captured two hundred Yankee cavalry at Strasburg.

Wednesday, March 4th — Cloudy nearly all day. Aunt Rebecca left for home today. Mother and Maggie went with her and returned this afternoon. Today is the second anniversary since the Abolition President assumed his office. What a fatal day that was for the nation as we look back to those two years, a sad picture of the most horrible and bloody presents itself. So many have been unmercifully cut off the bloom of youth and manhood to satisfy the passions of a craven despotic faction. Our Vicksburg boys have captured another ironclad, the *Indianianola*. Our President, Jefferson Davis, has issued a proclamation setting apart the 27th of this month as a day of fasting and prayer to return thanks to that Kind Heavenly Father who has alone, given us the victory.

Thursday, March 5th — Very cold and clear. We spent the day with Victoria. Eddie went with us. Lizzie was to have gone with us but was prevented from doing so on account of being sick. Victoria came by with us in the evening and has gone to see Lizzie.

Friday, March 6th — The wind was blowing hard all day, but lulled greatly this afternoon. Victoria returned home this afternoon. No news that we can hear. Par sent for a paper but did not succeed in getting one.

Saturday, March 7th — Clouds all day. Pattie came over this morning, and she is with us tonight. Par went to Hampton today and brought us a paper, in which is stated, a burning of the steamer Nashville (Confederate).

Sunday, March 8th — Cloudy soon this morning and commenced thundering about eight o'clock, the rain poured very fast. Pattie went home this morning. Sister and myself went to see Lizzie this afternoon. When we got there she was not at home, but returned not very long afterward. Mrs. Cooke and Lizzie came home with us. Lizzie is going to remain all night with us.

Monday, March 9th — Clear, in the morning, and remained so untill about 4 in the afternoon when the sky became somewhat cloudy. Lizzie left this morning after breakfast. I finished a worsted mat for Mother today.

Tuesday, March 10th — A rainy day. Uncle Kit came over and brought us a paper. The Confederate steamer Retribution has captured several prizes and some of them have been conveyed to Confederate Ports. Gen. VanDorn has had a fight with the Yankees in Tennessee which resulted in a Victory for our arms, he killed or captured three of the Yankee regiments.

Wednesday, March 11th — Cloudy this morning, also rain, but the clouds cleared away towards noon. The remainder of the day has been bright. There is no news.

Thursday, March 12th — Has been quite changeable some times snowing and again the sun shining. Uncle Kit brought us a paper but there is not any news of importance. Cousin Sallie moved today. Bettie Wade is coming to keep house for Uncle

Kit, I am very glad of it. Mr. and Mrs. Chandler were here this afternoon.

Friday, 13th. — Clear and cold, there is not any news. Sister and myself went to Mrs. Cooke's about 4 P. M. to carry Lizzie her crochet needle which she was kind enough to lend me.

Saturday, March 14th — Clear and cold. Today was Levin's birthday, he is sixteen years old. There is no news reliable.

Sunday, March 15th — Cloudy and cold. Levin carried us to Cousin Sarah's. We spent the morning with Cousin Sarah, and went over to Aunt Mollie's this afternoon. Cousin Anna came home with us.

Monday, March 16th — Cloudy and cold, there is not any news.

Tuesday, March 17th — Clear and mild. Cousin Anna and myself went to see Cousin Elvie, we called by Mrs. Cooke's and Lizzie went with us. We received a paper today in which it is reported that there has been a fight on the Yazoo river, and it is reported the Yankees have captured eight transports and seven thousand of our men but I do not believe it. It is also reported that Fort Doneldson and Fort Henry have been captured by us.

Wednesday, March 18th — Cloudy all day. I am eighteen today. As I look back to the last two years, I see many a treasured moment which I could fondly recall if in my power to do so, also many bright hopes wasted, blasted by the stern hand of unyielding fate, and is it thus? Yes my sad moments are known only to myself, and I hardly know myself until I read bygones deeply. It is my wish and prayer, that I may be happier and surrounded by absent friends ere my birthday shall again roll around, should I be spared to see it. Lizzie and Eddie were here this afternoon.

Thursday, March 19th — Cloudy. About half past ten A.M. it commenced snowing and this afternoon it snowed so hard as to cover the ground.

Friday, March 20th — Snowing still, it has been snowing all day, and it is very deep.

Saturday, March 21st — It has been raining nearly all day, still cloudy.

Sunday, March 22d — The clouds cleared away this morning and the remainder of the day has been clear. I heard today of the death of Tom Wise, he was sick only two days. This teaches us how frail we are, and should be a warning to us to be always ready to meet our God.

Monday, March 23d — Clear, the ground still very wet.

Tuesday, March 24th — Cloudy a greater part of the day. I walked over to Mrs. Cooke's this morning to review arithmetic with Lizzie. Cousin Anna went home. Sister and Levin carried us. Aunt Mollie came with them.

Wednesday, March 25th — Not very clear. I went to Mrs. Cooke's this morning.

Thursday, March 26th — Clear. I went over to Mrs. Cooke's this morning and Mother and Aunt Mollie went to see Cousin Elvie, and returned this afternoon.

Friday, March 27th — Clear and cold. Today was the day appointed by President Davis for fasting and prayer. Many an humble petition has ascended from true hearts devoted to one of the most sacred causes on earth, that of shielding their homes from the tyrannical sway of a most despotic foe. I trust our prayers may find response at a throne of grace for from Him (Our Heavenly Father) we must look for comfort. I see an account in one of the Yankee papers where they sent 5000 armed negroes to incite other slaves, and arm them for insurrection upon defenseless women and children, 1000 of them ascended St. Mary's river in Georgia commanded by Col. Higginson and Montgomery. It is believed they have fallen in the hands of our soldiers. I pray they have. Sister, Lizzie, Eddie and myself went to see Bettie Wade.

Saturday, March 28th — Cloudy all the morning. I went to Mrs. Cooke's this morning. Par went to Hampton today. It poured down raining this afternoon and he got very wet. We received a paper in which is a Southern account of the Yankee repulse at Port Hudson and Fort Pemberton, and the Yankees are in full retreat from Yazoo Pass. Gen. Banks' army is reported falling back, deserters are constantly coming into our lines of defenses on the Mississippi. There has been a cavalry fight at Brentwood, Tenn. Our forces, commanded by VanDorn and those of the Yankees by Smith. The fight was favourable to us, Smith being obliged to retreat. Truly.

Sunday, March 29th — Cold and cloudy, but it became brighter towards noon. I went home with Aunt Mollie. Home and brought Aunt Becca back with me. Mother went to Cousin Lizzie Woods. I received a letter from Mollie Curtis.

Monday, March 30 — Clear and cold. I went to Mrs. Cooke's this morning. Sister went to Mrs. King's this afternoon.

Tuesday, March 31st — Raining all the morning but cleared off in the latter part of the afternoon. Aunt Rebecca and Sister made our carpet and put it down this afternoon.

Wednesday, April 1st — Clear and very cold, the wind has been blowing hard all day. Mr. Hudgins and Uncle Kit sat with us until after nine o'clock P.M.

Thursday, April 2d — Clear and mild. I went to Mrs. Cooke's this morning.

Friday, April 3d — Cloudy and cold all day. Sister and myself spent this afternoon with Lizzie, she came home with us and remained all night. Uncle Kit was here when we got from Mrs. Cooke's.

Saturday, April 4th — Cloudy, the wind blowing very hard. Lizzie left this morning. It commenced snowing this afternoon and it is snowing quite fast now. I should so much like to know if our dear boys are sheltered from this storm. May the eye of a merciful Father look smilingly upon them and Angels gently guard their slumbers.

Sunday, Apr 5th — Cloudy the first part of the day but cleared away towards noon. Uncle Kit spent the day here.

Monday, Apr 6th — Clear, the Sun shining very warmly. Mother, Aunt Rebecca, Maggie and myself went to Cousin Sarah's and spent the day. We called by Aunt Mollie's this afternoon. Cousin Anna was quite sick, we had to leave Aunt Rebecca behind, I am very sorry. Cousin Sarah made me a present of a Bible, and advised me to profit by its Holy precepts, which I hope I may.

We received a paper this afternoon, in which is an account of their (the Yankee defeat) at Port Hudson. How thankful we should be to an All Wise Creator for smiling graciously upon our every effort.

Tuesday, April 7th — Clear in the morning but a little cloudy in the afternoon. Bettie spent the day with us. Lizzie came over in the afternoon.

Wednesday, April 8th — Clear. We spent the day at Uncle Frank's. Mollie Curtis was there and we brought her home with us.

Thursday, April 9th — Clear. There is no news of importance.

Friday, April 10th — Clear and mild. Sister, Mollie and myself spent the day with Bettie. Mollie is going to remain all (night) with Bettie. I saw a newspaper today in which is stated a Yankee disaster on the Teche, La. The Yankee Gen. Forest has been cut off from Newbern, N. C. The Gunboat *Lancaster* has been destroyed and the *Diana* captured by our forces. It is said the Confederate steamer *Natchez* has been destroyed.

Saturday, April 11th — Clear. The cannonading towards Williamsburg this morning was quite heavy. This afternoon we learned that the Confederates were in Williamsburg and captured several hundred Yankees.

Sunday, April 12th — Today has been similar to yesterday. Mollie came home this afternoon. I was delighted to see her. Mother went for Aunt Rebecca this morning.

Monday, April 13th — Cloudy a greater part of the day. Vic spent the day with us. We went to walk with her and got frightened on the way home.

Tuesday, April 14th — Clear. Mother and Aunt Rebecca went to Cousin William's and spent the day, we remained at home. Lizzie came in the afternoon. Cannonading has been heavy throughout the day.

Thursday, April 16th — A beautiful morning, but the afternoon was quite cloudy. Uncle Kit brought us a paper this evening. The Yankees have been repulsed at Charleston and their operations are coming on very slowly on the Mississippi. It is reported we have sunk one Yankee ironclad and taken one on the Nansemond River.

Friday, April 17th — A bright morning. Aunt Rebecca and Sister spent the day at Mrs. Cooke's and Mollie and myself spent the day at Cousin Sallie's. We had quite an agreeable day. Our forces are in possession of Williamsburg.

Saturday, April 18th — A clear day. Mother and Aunt Rebecca spent the day at Mrs. Presson's. We received a paper this afternoon. The Yankee fleet has left Charleston.

Sunday, April 19th — A clear bright day — Sister, Mollie and myself went to Cousin Sallie's this morning but did not remain long. It is reported our forces have surrounded Suffolk. I hope it is so. There has been heavy cannonading going on this afternoon and still continues now and it is night. They are roaring away whilst I am writing. I am all anxiety to hear from it.

Monday, April 20th — Cloudy. Sister, Mollie and myself spent the day with Victoria. We had quite a nice time. It poured down raining all the afternoon and Dr. King sent us home.

Tuesday, April 21st — Cloudy and cold. No news of importance.

Wednesday, April 22d — A little cloudy. Mollie went to Uncle Kit's this morning. Sister and myself went with her but returned to dinner.

Thursday, April 23d — A pouring rain all the morning but it slacked up this afternoon. Uncle Kit spent the day here. He brought me a note from Mollie. I answered it and sent the articles she requested me to send.

Friday, Apr 24th — Cloudy all day.

Saturday, Apr 25 — Clear, the wind blowing quite hard. I planted flower seed in my garden this morning.

Sunday, April 26th — A bright day. Cousin Lizzie Wood and Hannah spent the day with us. We received a newspaper in which it stated that six gunboats and three transports passed our batteries on the night of the 17th at Vicksburg and it is also stated that the Yankee Gen. Foster is in pursuit of the Confederate Gen. Hill.

Monday Apr. 27th — A bright mild day. Mother went to Mrs. Cooke's and spent the afternoon. Lizzie came home with her and remained all night with us.

Tuesday, April 28th — Cloudy all day accompanied by slight showers of rain. Lizzie left this morning.

Wednesday, April 29th — Still continues cloudy. No news of any importance.

Thursday, April 30th — Raining all the morning but it slackened this afternoon and the sun set clear. Bettie came this afternoon to remain all night to go after snails tomorrow. Mollie came also.

Friday, May 1st — Clear sweet day. All of us arose and went after snails, each of us were lucky enough to find one. We got back before sunrise and put our snails in plates of meal. The initials in my plate were A,O, as nearly as I understood them. At twelve o'clock we looked down the well but none of us were fortunate enough to see anything. Bettie's Grandpa came for her this afternoon. Mollie went home with her. Mother went to Aunt Mollie's and Cousin Sarah this afternoon. They were well at both places with the exception of Cousin Sarah who has a cold.

Saturday, May 2d — Such a calm sweet day. It seems as if indeed we are upon the verge of summer, trees are putting their buds and leaves, and all nature seems as if putting on its robes of bright and gorgeous colors. Each day brings to our minds the many blessings that have been bestowed by a gracious Father upon man. Many, ah, very many that were here to greet the month of flowers, twelve months back, are now sleeping in their lowly beds. Sad and sickening is the thought.

Sunday, May 3d — Similar to yesterday. We received a newspaper today in which is stated that four transports are known to have been sunk attempting to pass the Vicksburg batteries. Our forces, a detachment of cavalry, have made a raid on the Baltimore and Ohio Railroad tearing up the track, rendering unfit for travel until repaired. Bettie and Miss Martha brought Mollie back this afternoon. Little Levin carried her down to

Uncle Frank's where she intends teaching school. Lizzie came over this afternoon.

Monday, May 4th — The anniversary of the evacuation of Yorktown by our forces. How sad then were my feelings to know it was no longer in our possession. But thanks to an ever Merciful Providence, our young Confederacy has woven for its heritage immortal honor, our brave and truehearted sons have met, baffled, and defeated armies (who thought themselves invincible) whose heart was filled with vengeance to wreak upon "The Southern Rebels" and at once make them vassals, disregardless of the laws of civilized nations. But the Lord of Hosts has been with us, and given us help from trouble for which all hearts should never cease to give thanks.

Tuesday, May 5th — Clear the first part of the day. Mrs. Cooke and Lizzie came over this afternoon. About sunset it com—menced to rain a little and Mrs. Cooke remained with us. Lizzie went home. There has been a heavy cloud tonight.

Wednesday, May 6th — Still cloudy and it seems as if it will continue for some time.

Thursday, May 7th — Similar to yesterday.

Friday, May 8th — Cloudy and cool. Uncle Kit came over this morning and made an engagement to carry us to see Aunt Mollie and Cousin Sarah. We went this afternoon and found them all well. Uncle Kit seemed to enjoy himself very much. It is reported in the Yankee papers that there has been a severe battle at Fredericksburg and that the loss was great on both sides. They say they captured Fredericksburg and then our brave and indomitable came up and retook. I put not much faith in this for I think they have met with a disastrous repulse. I hope my surmise may prove a true one.

Saturday, May 9th — The clouds cleared away this morning and it has been a lovely day. Mrs. Cooke left for home this afternoon. We have again repulsed the Yankee Gen. Hooker.

Sunday, May 10th — Clear. Mother rode up to Aunt Mollie's this afternoon and Mrs. Crandol came here this afternoon.

Monday, May 11th — Clear and warm.

Tuesday, May 12th —— Clear and warm. It is said that Gen. Jackson is wounded in the left arm and it had to be amputated.

Wednesday, May 13th — Still continues warm. Sister went to Mrs. Cooke's this afternoon.

Thursday, May 14th —— Clear in the morning but it became cloudy late in the afternoon and we had a shower of rain last night.

Friday, May 15th —— Clear and cool. Sister and myself went to see Cousin Elvie this afternoon. We came home about dark. Uncle brought us a paper, in which is an account of the battle of Saturday and Sunday of the 2d and 3d of May near Fredericksburg, in which paper there are extracts from our papers, in which it is said the loss was heavy on both sides. Our loss amounting to six or seven thousand and that of the Yankees from twenty—five or thirty thousand. It is now said that Gen. Jackson is dead. I hope it is not true for it seems such a pity to lose a brave hero as our Jackson, truly nobly he has served his sunny South, and if he is dead, all will deeply feel and deplore his loss. I hope that our Kind Heavenly Father will protect and bless with Victory our noble Southerners. We should all thank Him for the Victory He hath given us.

Saturday, May 16th — Clear all the forenoon, but it became cloudy late in the afternoon. Par went fishing today. This afternoon we had a nice dish of fresh fish for dinner.

Sunday, May 17th —— Cloudy early in the morning but the clouds soon cleared away, and the day was quite clear. Levin carried Sister and myself to see Cousin Lizzie. We spent the day with her.

Monday, May 18th — Still clear and cool. Par was taken with a chill last night and he is much indisposed today. Mother went for Cousin Sarah this afternoon. She is coming to spend a short time with us.

Tuesday, May 19th — Clear bright day. Mother and Cousin Sarah went to Mrs. Crandol's but she was not at home. We had a nice joke on them. Sister and myself spent the afternoon with Victoria. Lizzie was there also.

Wednesday, May 20th — A bright warm day. Mother and Cousin Sarah went to Mrs. Cooke's this morning, returned home to dinner. Sister and myself went to Mrs. Cooke's late in the after-noon, and Lizzie came home with us and remained all night.

Thursday, May 21st — Clear and very warm. Sister, Lizzie and I went to see Cousin Elvie this morning and while there we looked down the well. Lizzie and all of us thought we saw a man's image down in the well, her future husband, I suppose. In the afternoon we went to Mrs. Buchanan's and spent the afternoon. When we returned home we found Cousin Sarah quite sick.

Friday, May 22d — Very warm. I see an account in the papers where Public speakers in the city of New York are denouncing Lincoln's administration. They are aroused by the arresting of Mr. Vallandigham of Ohio and speak of rising up to resist the draft.

Saturday, May 23d — Clear and very warm. Cousin Sarah was sick again today. Mrs. Cooke spent the day with us. Mr. Segar made a speech today at the tabernacle. It seems as if they are going to guide the people entirely by Yankee rule.

Sunday, May 24th — Similar to yesterday. Cousin Sarah went home this afternoon. Victoria, Lizzie, Kit and Teddie spent the afternoon here. Sister and myself went home with Lizzie and remained all night.

Monday, May 25th — I returned home this afternoon. The weather is cloudy and cool.

Tuesday, May 26th — Still cloudy and cool. Several Yankees came here today in search of one of their horses.

Wednesday, May 27th — Clear. Mollie and Aunt Sarah spent the afternoon here. Mollie, Sister and I rode to see Bettie, and staid a short while.

Thursday, May 28th — Clear and pleasant. An Election was opened at the Halfway House, for members of Congress.

Friday, May 29th — Clear all the morning. It clouded up late this afternoon but the clouds soon wore away.

Saturday, May 30th — Cloudy all day. Par went fishing this morning and caught a nice parcel of fish. Lizzie came over about four o'clock and remained until after supper. Sister, Maggie, and I walked with her when she went home.

Sunday, May 31st — Clear and warm. Sister and Mother went to Aunt Mollie's this morning, they found all well. Oh, that such beautiful Sabbaths could be spent in a holier way than battling and preparing for battle, but our places of worship have been demolished and there is now not more than two churches where services can be held.

Monday, June 1st — Clear and pleasant. Aunt Sarah and Mollie came yesterday and I went home with them.

Tuesday, June 2d — I returned home this afternoon from Uncle Frank's. I had a nice time while there practicing riding horseback. We received a paper and the Yankees have again been repulsed at Vicksburg.

Wednesday, June 3d — Cloudy accompanied by showers of rain. I went to Mrs. Cooke's this afternoon. Whilst there, three Yankees came and searched the kitchen for arms. On returning home I found they had been here also.

Thursday, June 4th — Clear. We received a paper today in which has late news from Vicksburg, two desperate assaults had been made in which the Yankees were repulsed with great loss. In less than 30 minutes 2500 men were killed or wounded. We have also sunk the gunboat *Cincinnati*, this occured on the 23d of May. How grateful we should be for such success, to that Giver Who seems as if delivering us from those that would crush us, down to the very dust.

Friday, June 6th — Clear and pleasant.

Saturday, June 6th — Clear and exceedingly pleasant.

Sunday, June 7th — Clear. There is no news of importance. Laura and Uncle Barnie came by here, on their way home.

Monday, June 8th — Clear and pleasant. Mollie, Aunt Sarah and Mrs. Curtis came here this afternoon, they walked all the way from home. Sister went home with them. Lizzie and Victoria came by this afternoon. Lizzie remains all night with me.

Tuesday, June 9th — Everything calm and mild. Sister returned home this afternoon.

Wednesday, June 10th — Still clear.

Thursday, June 11th — Cloudy in the morning but the clouds cleared away in a short time. Lizzie came here this afternoon, we walked to see Bettie. We received a paper tonight. The Yankees seem confident, or trying to make persons believe they are in the capture of Vicksburg.

Friday, June 12th — Clear and pleasant this morning. Mother went to Mrs. Cooke's and returned to dinner. Late this afternoon it clouded up and rained a shower.

Saturday, June 13th — Pleasant and clear. Yes, everything seems so very mild in all nature, but let us think awhile, and we see the dark visitant, War, hanging over our sunny land, spreading death and devastation.

Sunday, June 14th — Cloudy all day. Uncle Barnie and Laura spent the day here. Mollie and Mrs. Curtis came by here this morning.

Monday, June 15th — Clear and warm. There is no news of importance.

Tuesday, June 16th — Clear and very warm.

Wednesday, Jun 17th — Clear and warm. Three Yankees came here this afternoon and searched the house. They carried Par and his gun to Mr. Bartlett's with them. I suppose he sent them here to search for his goods, a very cheap way of calling a man a rogue. It is an epithet which has never been applied before to any of the Smith family, but we cannot expect to find a gentleman in the person of one so base as he.

Thursday, June 18th — Clear and warm.

Friday, June 19th — Rainy this morning, it was quite refreshing. We have received a paper. Gen. Lee is invading Md. and Penna. Vicksburg still holds out bravely.

Saturday, June 20th — Cloudy all day. Laura came by here on her way to Mrs. Garrow's.

Friday, July 10th — Several weeks have lapsed since I penned any in my journal, quite a number of changes have taken place within that brief period. Battles have been fought in which the Yankee's say we are defeated, yet we cannot tell, for they are ever ready to say so. Many a brave hero has sunk into their last long sleep, far away from home. Yet how noble did they fall contending for everything that makes life a blessing.

Friday, August 21st — More than a month has intervened since I last wrote in this little book. Since then we have met with reverses. Vicksburg is no longer ours. Gen. Lee has invaded the North, and we have been checked by some mismanagement, yet I do not repine, nor shall I ever, as long as an army or our land remains. Our men are still brave and resolute, and many more are willing to sacrifice their precious lives in the cause for liberty or death, and defense of the sanctity of our Southern homes and the fair daughters of our land are as willing as ever to toil. We pray for our heroes, as they were when our Stars and Bars were first unfurled and displayed to the Southern breeze. Many of us have been made to mourn the loss of friends, yet willingly do we resign them, although the parting is severe, and what is worse, they have fallen by the hands of our invaders, when we consider that they have perished in defense of the noblest cause that has ever stirred the breast of man. Today has been set apart by our President as a day of fasting and prayer. Many a petition has been offered up at a Throne of Grace in behalf of our cause. I wish we could have had some place of worship where to assemble.

Monday, Sept 20th 1863 — O how sad and lonely I sometimes feel, yes, unhappy. Little doth the passerby know how or why one over whose head only 18 summers have passed so swiftly with its joys and sorrows should thus complain. No, for my little troubles are confessed chiefly to mine own bosom. I, having no Confidante into whose ears to breath my feelings with the exception of this little book, and it is not often I pen them here. I have this morning been perusing some letters, penned by one whose hand is cold in death, and over whose breast the cold, cold sod now forms a covering of that breast which so full of life and patriotism now lies smouldering in the dust and with many a bright hopes, now fled forever, and why so? O rebellious heart, be still, the parting is past. Why should I wish to recall him back to this Land of strife from the Arms of Jesus where he is sweetly reposing where all earthly scenes must pass into the stream of oblivion. Yet I cannot forget, would that I could. I review the past with deep regrets. Oh My Father, if I complain too much, forgive, for I am a child of earth.

Friday; Oct 24th 1863 — A pouring rain, just such a one that forms a mood for thinking. I wish I could get a letter but it seems as if it is almost vain to wish. I never receive one from Jennie but what it carries me back to the times we used to spend together, and it always makes me sad but I do love so dearly to read them, there is so much to console and comfort me penned by her. Well the time is rapidly approaching if life lasts for me to come to some decision. I must think well and think deeply, more than I have in the last week or so or I shall perhaps find the time for thinking no longer mine, and it may not be right for me to keep another so long in expectance. I almost dread the time to come, but come it must, sooner or later. I have limited it to a shorter period than I expected. I know it will cost me some sad moments anyhow for I cannot help respecting the feelings of others when I am confident they are sincere.

* * * * *

Jan. 14th 1864 —— Just this night two years ago, how long and
dreary it seems since that time, and oh, how many changes
since that happy period. As memory bears me back, how many
a sigh of regret heaves my breast, a sigh for the past and its
hallowed associations, around which clusters so many youthful
dreams now forever fled. Lightly did every pulsation of my
heart seem this night only two short years past. All around
enlivened and cheered fond hearts beat in unison that are now
cold in the embrace of death. Every glance betokened love,
hope, and joy. The sounds of festivity broke sweetly upon my
ear, and the voice of loved ones gave a charm to conversation.
No pang of sorrow found its way to my girlish heart, no dark
shadows flittered among my fond imagineings. All spoke peace
within although War was devastating our Sunny Land. Yet I
knew it only by name, it had not touched my daydreams, but
it came at last. It separated me from those who loved me and
now where are they? Some dead, slain upon the battlefields
contending for home and liberty. There they rest quietly,
sweetly, where no war drum can arouse them, and no vandal
would disturb their quiet repose. They who are now sleeping
on that battle plain were by my side this night only two years
ago in all pride and glow of manhood. But now, ah, sad and
sickening thought, they have fled from earth, stricken down
by the hand of the cruel vandal, and they are now with the
departed.

Feb 3d 1864 —— I don't know why or what has come over my feelings
of late. It seems as if all desire for visiting has vanished and I
scarcely feel right anywhere else but here, where my lone
thoughts are far dearer a companion to me than anything else.
Is it the old sad forebodings visiting again my once happy
heart? I had thought I had learned in a measure to control
myself when thinking of past memories, sweet bygones, perhaps forgotten by all save me. Yet the wounded heart cannot
entirely forget it once suffered. O, let years roll on, the scars
will still be possible to its own posseser. I wonder if when our
friends pass from this world, if they are endowed with the fac-
ulty of remembering they once knew us and if they from their
celestial homes ever think of me here. Does their spirit ever

hover near me, here, if so do they love less because I am a weak
frail earthly being? I know I am weak or I could better bear
my heart up from the wages of sorrow that once visited. Few
will ever know how dark and dreary all around me then
seemed. Gladly would I hurl those moments of dispair into the
vortex of oblivion but a wise Providence has forbade that I
should quaff the stream of lithe, and I bend submissing yet I
sometimes fear I rebel against my better nature, and wish for
those who have departed. Yet tis wrong! for they are now resting sweetly peacefully free from earth's temptations, toils and
dangers. They have died the death of martyrs and the fair
chaplet of glory, it's the sweetest, finest gem that could be
asked to brighten the tomb.

February 15th 1864 — Oh how fast it is snowing. I can cast my eye
towards the window and see the pure white flecks falling very
fast and thick. I came up to get my work so I thought I would
write a few lines in my journal. Just then a heavy sigh, but
that is hardly noticed by any, save me. I sigh, yet I sometimes
"scarce know why" unless it is I feel lonely when contemplating
bygones, sweet bygones, that made themselves a very part of
my existance and which is the beacon that lures my imagination back, and I gaze and muse upon them hourly or I may so
daily. Yet they must remain as now. I cannot recall them for
they have fled and each day finds them receding farther into
the past, yet as vivid as ever to my youthful mind as when I
first knew their winning influence. What could we not do sometimes if it were not for the scorn with which we are apt to meet
at the hands of this false, fair world? Many a consoling word
would be uttered that must remain dormant. I sometimes am
almost ready to say I will write her, then comes the thought
perhaps other lips than hers will peruse my letter, and I might
at once be called a presumptious girl. Yet I feel it almost a duty
imposing upon me to offer her my sympathy, for I know she
knew he loved me, but would it touch some wound in her
stricken heart causing it to bleed afresh? If so, I would not for
the world give her one moment's pain, but if my sympathy
would be of any solace to her then gladly would I be influenced

only by the consoling thought I can comfort her and I would obey only the dictates of my warm true heart.

Sunday Feb 21st 1864 — All have gone out and I am left entirely alone, no, not entirely for have I not my thoughts to keep myself company? Yes, they my constant companions are still with me and as busy as ever, scanning the blight made by the present which is obscured by the clouds of what may be called sorrow. I feel sometimes almost desolate at heart when I think of those who loved and lost above, when I think or know they have departed never more to visit fair, fair earth again, never more to smile upon me with looks of love and contentment. Yet they have acted the part of patriots, have gravely breathed away their lives in freedom's cause. They have set a noble example for their comrades, and maintained that motto which characterizes every Southern heart ("We conquer or die") and though I know all this, yet the heart somehow will feel its wounds bled afresh when thinking of the departed. Yet they have acted as I would have them for I would scorn to see them shrink from upholding the banner of a bleeding aggravated Country. My Heavenly Father I will not murmur at thy dispensations, for thou hast still left one to toil on for his home of whom I am proud to call my Cousin. It shall be my ardent prayer that he may be spared to see the foes of his country banished from our Sunny Land. Man is a strange creature. I wonder they say. I sometimes think they do, and their ways countermand this though — and I am almost ready to if they mean half what then again some of believe they scarcely know the true meaning of all they say themselves.

Saturday, March 5th 1864 — I have just come up from ironing. I feel weary, sad and almost lonely. I sit meditating, I see early anticipations fled from my path, dispersed by the hand of unrelenting fate. I feel as if hardly a sunbeam shines. Lo, light to dark portals through which a gladdening light has long since ceased to glow. Ah none but me has ever trod its silent way. The rain is pouring in torrents which sounds really sweet to me.

March 19, 1864 — Yesterday was my birthday. It hardly seems prob-
able that nineteen years have elapsed since a little infant was
ushered into this busy bustling world. Yet it is so and if no dark
war had sighed itself over our sunny land, I could hardly realize that I was that old, for I think when the river of one's life
flows only happily that they feel much younger than when its
waves are maddened by the torrent of troubles and disappointments. I wonder if I shall feel much happier my next birthday
if I am living than now. I hope so for by that time I hope our
Southern homes will be prospering under the blessings of peace
and those that are battling in defence of our Country may
return to the hearts of friends and kindred. I am sometimes
addressed by the familiar epithet of "Old Lady." Perhaps I
seem old to them. Yet they know not how deeply my heart has
been touched, when listening silently to the rehearsal of the
death of some loved one who has perished away from those who
loved them. Like the dew that leaves the summer flowers after
being exposed to the burning rays of the summer's sun, so fades
the smiles from the lip when thinking of those that have been
thus cruelly wronged.

March 25th 1864 — The winds sigh mournfully past my window as
I sit alone in my room penciling a few lines in this little book.
Perhaps they have listed awhile and hovered around the mound
of some silent sleeper, who is unconscious of their breathings
and who has in a measure been forgotten by some. Yet there
is a heart, although humble it be, that wafts a sigh to the passing breeze and fain would have it bourne swiftly to the silent
one, and ere long sweet spring flowers will begin to bloom and
seem in instructive language to say "I'll watch thy slumbers,
though they are those of death." My heart feels sad and it
seems as if the very breezes speak to my soul in their low mur-
murings and tell me my heart is indeed lonely for there is no
cherished image concealed in it, but only a shadow dim that
tells too well what once was, but is it not better thus? For are
not some bettered by the change? I sometimes try to think so
but then a sigh of regret involuntarily heaves my breast which
should never murmur of a Divine Will yet there would never

come a rebellious regret if the past could be forgotten. No, it must not, cannot be, howsoever it may be desired.

April 1st 1864 — I am sitting alone in my silent chamber musing upon the beautiful bright long ago. The rain falls softly sometimes pattering against the panes and seems as forming an accompaniment for my musings, that I move sadly through my mind, indelibly stamped with the image of those who acted a principal part in the heart's drama. Yes, swiftly flies my thoughts back and a saddening memory comes stealing gently o'er me bringing with it those that have passed from the stage of this life to rest in the lone dark and silent sepulchre of the dead. Again in my imagination are they before as of old, yet only for a moment and it is gone. Reality banishes the fond delusion, and leaves the heart as bare of a cherished affection as if it had never known that such a gem existed. For now it must cherish toward those who are gone, only that love which belongs to those who are with the sainted dead. Do they think of and pray for me? There is a thought which has often suggested itself to mind. Yet I suppose not, for in that Blest abode no thought of earthly objects dim the luster of a mind absolutely happy.

> *"Oh, earth, earth, earth, with thy mocking skies*
> *of blue, where would the weary find repose were there no*
> *Risen Lord, no guarded tomb, no Gethsemane.*
>
> *"In almost every heart there is a sepulchre*
> *as well as a garland of life's choicest flowers."*

Miss Mary O. Smith
York-County.

* * * * *

April 4, 1865 — A year has elapsed since last I engraved my pensive
thoughts on the sheets of this little book, and today I sit saddened and almost despairing. Our own Loved and long
contested for City has fallen. Can it, must it be. Oh, it seems as
if I cannot bear the thought to know so many young and gallant hearts have fallen in its defense and now at last the
oppressors foot tread those walks, that not long since echoed
to the footfalls of our own brave men, and now at last the spot
that contains the remains of some. Many of her sons are desecrated by the shouts of a victorious enemy. Oh, if they could
know, how could they rest beneath their turf grown homes
where they have slept guarded from harm by brave comrades.
If in their bright homes above they cannot be conscious or they
could not rest in peace.

Levin, Bob and Eddie commenced school 6th of February,
received payment. Paid up to July

Bennie commenced 13th of Feb. Johnny Cook 27th of March

Ella Partrick com. 1st of May, Martha and Billie 12th of June,
Mollie and Willie, 13th of June, Bettie and Kit, 15th of June,
Mollie Ray, 19th of June, Johnnie Watson commenced school
10th of July, Willie Wainwright commenced school 10th of July.
Levin, Bob and Eddie com. 6th of July

Maggie L. Smith, Mary O. Smith, Levin G. Smith R T B

My heart draws in every thought connected with him. I know I
loved him truly, deeply, alas, too deeply for any being to love
anything so transient as life. I love, I revere his memory. I can
scarcely resign myself to think tis all for the best. I know not
how sincerely I did love until all was o'er. With him I would have
rather walked hand in hand through life's rugged most thorny
pathways, occuppying my place in his true and noble heart than
to reign unrivalled queen of any other land or dwell in Eden's
bower. There is something in the deep devotion of a woman's
love which it is impossible to comprehend. Nothing but death
can extinguish the feeling with which she regards him on whom
she has placed her affection. He may treat her with coldness and
indifference but her undying affection will win it all should he
be disappointed by the world. If he will turn to her in his mis-
fortunes he is sure to find a refuge and a comforter. When all

these ply him, it is only in misfortune that her affections can be appreciated. A woman's love will endure forever, it is her world, her all! Destroy it and her happiness has departed, never again to return!!

And death, no, even death cannot extinguish the love for him, for deep in my heart there is a grave. No grass grows there, no sunbeam sheds its rays above the mound. It is enveloped by the veil of the past — the irrevocable past.

First Lessons in French for Children by Mrs. Barbault.

Pinney Exercises with Key.

* * * * *

March 18, 1866 — My birthday, I have been spared to see twenty—one years with its dangers and temptations roll o'er me. A gratuitous Father has led me safely along through my past life, and now as I stand upon the eve of a maturer life opening for me, I look back with a sigh of regret. Life has had for me its joys as well as its sorrows. I feel as if I can never feel that same ardent heart thrilling sensation as in the long ago. My heart has been deeply touched by that delightful sensation that all in the course of life are apt to know. Yet why was it so! better, far better had it never have been. Alas, the waters of love were only agitated to leave behind them a dry and barren waste. Oh, my God, may it not always be so. May I not find some heart to which my own can respond. A whisper! Answer, No! No! there is none like him.

July 5, 1866 — The Picnic of the fourth is over. I enjoyed it very much, danced, chatted and was gay generally. I received in the course of the evening a piece of advice from one of my gentle—men friends which I hope will be a great benefit to me in the future. It has changed the whole tenor of my actions. I shall adopt the plan he suggests, though it be painful to another. Yet I feel it a duty I owe to myself and him. I never intend if I can help it without downright insult to his feelings to allow him to wait on me again. Perhaps he will think it strange but I cannot help it. That hour's conversation has changed the light frivolous feelings of the girl into a determined woman, a deter-mination to act and let them all see how they are deceived. I wish him much happiness and hope that he may form some new attachments, where he will be far happier and his hopes related to me been realized. I cannot love him and therefore must not ever think of marrying him. I feel deeply also. None knows how deeply I do feel and appreciate his love which I am conscious of it in every glance of his eye, every tone of his voice. Yet he must, know all and that soon then my plans shall go on as I have portrayed them in my own imagination.

July 13th 1866 — I feel wounded and depressed in spirit. The heart is weak, clinging ever dependent upon others for sympathy, crush that sympathetic feeling and at once looses all of its youthful gladness. Ah, life is dreary, waste, a void, through which we blindly grope our way. Sneers, scoffs and blighting tunes meet us on every hand. Those who often should be the very ones to make all sunshine often by their impetuosity, roll back instead the cold dark waves to wash away every sunbeam on life's ocean. Why were some of us poor mortals constructed so as to feel so sensibly every thoughtless, dont careish remark? Wherein does it benefit us to be so sensitive? Yet I cannot help it, I feel a dull heavy sad feeling. All seems a void, no animating hopes, no bright gleams thru the future's mystic veil. But should I repine? No, No. Many others have far greater cause for such feelings.

* * * * *

February 18th 1867 —— My feelings of vanity, if there exists any in
my girlish heart would have surely been elated yesterday, when
I received that short but expressive note. Many thanks for the
high opinion both of my dear friends entertain for me. I appreciate them and sincerely pray that I may be worthy of every
kind thought they entertain for fear that they overrate me. I
fear I am not all they claim for me. I try, if I sometimes fail, to
plod the path to duty and honor, though those duties may
sometimes be arduous. Yet there is where the glory lies. If every
day brought only pleasures, and labor light, where would be
the sacrifice where the satisfaction that anything had been
accomplished. Happy thought —— to know I have for one
moment cast the faintest shadow of trust in heart deceived and
weary. Where all the buoyant hopes of youth, gladdened by the
tone of one loved voice, were cruelly blighted by the same and
only one, who first thought that heart the song of love, which
woman, poor, weak, clinging, dependent woman, looks upon as
the Eden of her life, trusting too often only to be deceived by
man's treachery, that can conceal the monster deceit, while
breathing in some young and trusting ear, those vows which if
faithfully kept would perhaps have gladdened her future life
and clad driest garden with bright flowerets instead of thorns
and thistles. Well, M____ has found an ideal. Is A real, or only
a romance like the first proved? It is time she should know the
difference between the two, how ardently she will love if she
thinks the object worthy. May she see her dreams of all that is
great and good realized in him. It surely must be Cicero she
loves, he did not say. I must know whom it is, free did she say
I am. Surely she is not in every sense of the word, she cannot
be as she was when we last met. I did not think her just the
same. Ah! yes! I cannot but pity yet I do not think I love.
Those very attributes that would promote my love are lacking
but he truly has some noble qualities, his sensitiveness I must
say I admire. Some, I may have loved, but that dream is now
passed. It is the one great oasis in my past, to which I revere
with a melancholy pleasure. He was one to command the love
and respect of such a heart as mine. Noble, dignified, the very
soul of truth and honor, such alone is what my proud heart

aspires to. Although I may appear heartless to some, yet, I have a warm true heart that could love, and has devotedly. What am I saying? The truth is, I hardly know sometimes. I must have loved, when he was all I could ask. I must stop this confab and go to my work. The more I write, the more I wish to.

April 1st 1867 — Today two weeks ago was my 22nd birthday. I did not as it is usual write in this little book on that day as I spent the day from home. Answered Mollie's letter but have not received an answer as yet. Lizzie spent the night with me last night. We laid awake a considerable time talking. I feel sorry for her. I wish she would return the wealth of affection lavished on her devoted suitor, Mr. T__. Alas! I fear her affections are preengaged, where her girlish dreams can never be realized. She yielded, when she thought she was beloved in return, but I fear not. Those first impressions have cast a shadow that will not flee all over her youth, causing a dreary desolate blank which no voice but his who first awakened in her breast. Love's young dream can ever hush that weary sighing for love. I think would conquer. I could not love where it was not mutual, but we don't know. I pray it may never be my fate. I have no ideal on which to cast my affections, my earliest and best have fled, never, I fear, to be awakened by the thrilling tones of another. I could have after a while asked no greater bliss than to know such a heart as his was mine. God in his infinite mercy saw best, and took the Idol, ere the shrine was reared, to what it would have been. I might in all my absorbing love for him been forgetful who bestowed such blessings. Let me look calmly upon it, Oh, my God, for I fear I wrong another in speaking this even here for Oh! there was another that loved me deeply, truly, and I, ere my heart had scarcely emerged in womanhood thought I too loved but I fear it was not that deep devoted fervor, which woman can so pour out on the heart she deeply, truly loves. I gave him to know his love was mutual. I thought I loved but there came a pair of mournful expressive black eyes between us. The girlish dreams I formerly cherished seemed overthrown. God prevented me from casting a blight on either heart. He took them both away before the hour of trial came.

Oh, I cannot bear to know. I should have wounded his true
heart. I was his first and last, he said he never loved any but
me. I know he would not tell a falsehood, but I cannot write
more. My heart feels too deep even for words.

June 9th 1867 — When amid the gay and idle prattlers, who could
ever dream my feelings were ever more than superficial. Who
would suppose to see me then, that there still lives in my heart
a monument scarred, and sustained by me of past memories
and sacred associations that enshrine all that has been bright
and beautiful in my life, for which I would not barter for
untold wealth, for pearls, or gems of inestimable value. It is
what I gaze and feed my very soul upon in my sad moments.
The guiding star to which I turn when heartfelt and weary with
the toils of life and the heartless devil which presents itself,
turn where we will in this false world of ours, which seems so
fair and lures us on only to decay.

For we, yes, I may well say all of us, use to the very extent of
nature that is all—ways filled to the brim and o'er flowing with
that bitter commodity known in the language of the sterner sex
as Hypocracy. For without that essence to savor the would be
supposed truth that we always try to incense them to believe,
how should we get along? Mary Octavia.

August 13th 1867 — The more I think of what transpired last
evening, the more I am confounded and puzzled beyond measure. Nothing could have surprised me more, had a pistol or any
weapon been aimed at me in a malicious manner. It could not
have more astonished me than did that declaration coming
from his lips. I never imagined he loved, so well he acted his
part. I can only say I am not (have) so well acquainted with
human nature as I had flattered myself. He whom I had
deemed cold and almost invisible was in a moment changed to
a yielding affectionate man. I never knew I could exert so much
influence on a heart I had deemed stern and inflexible. I never
knew the deep quiet feeling that his heart cherished toward me
all through years of gloom and sorrow. Standing in the moonlight as he was about to leave, he looked so mild, so loverlike.
I could only gaze in silent wonder as he bade me goodbye at
the door. I always imagined his affections preengaged, how it

was he managed to conceal his real sentiments so long must with me forever remain a mystery that cannot be fathomed. He can mention the subject to me again, or not, just as best suits him. I fear he thought I encouraged him but I did not mean to do it. I felt so sorry for him I could not deprive him of the small pleasure of standing by my side, conversing in gentle tones. I hardly know what to think about the subject. I know he has a heart whose hidden depths have been stirred unconsciously by me. The leaves in my life's history are being slowly but surely unfolded. What will happen next? I am not surprised now at anything that may happen. I know I made an interesting picture, sitting, hardly knowing what to say, so overwhelmed with surprise. I wonder when I shall see him again. How will I converse with him now? In the same girlish strain? I do not know. I fear I may say or do something awkward. It has taught (me) to observe more closely next time. Well my little book is almost filled. Little did I expect ever to even know what is recorded here.

Saturday Nov 2nd 1867 —— Memory, sweet noiseless memory, how oft do you bear me back to happier days than now, when all was bright and beautiful in this life of ours, ere the storm of war had burst upon us or cruelly severed loved ones that this quiet beautiful November evening are sleeping calmly their last long quiet asleep in some lonely plain or on some lone deserted battle field. The golden sunbeams as they shine aslant the western sky have something sad in their gentle glow. My life, although seemingly but one short day, has seen its radiant morn rise clear and cloudless, but ere the noon came, the storm came forth, causing a void in my warm young heart. For, Oh I know I must have loved, or I could not now repine. God, Oh my God, grant the evening of my life may close doing thy will, waiting on thee, rejoicing in thy glory. May I learn to do thy will and meekly bow whenever thou seem fit to chasten.

* * * * *

This begins in the middle of an entry in the continuation of the diary of Mary Octavia Smith Tabb in January 1868.

... lively as possible, all of (us) ate egg and salt hoping to see the partner of our joys and sorrows.

Wednesday, Jan 15, 1868 — Not one of us was blessed with a vision of our future companions. Lizzie is with me again tonight, the earth has been a perfect sleet all day. Sir John left about sunset this evening, he tried to see how he could worry us before he left by rumpling our hair. He is a great tease when he chooses. I would that I could read aright my own heart, but alas! I find myself incompetent to the task. Of one thing I am sure that is I am beloved. I feel sorry and feel a tender regard for every kindly glance, word or act. Ah too truly is the secret revealed to me, I know all too well. Received a letter from Jennie today. She sent me her photograph which I prize very highly.

Thursday, Jan 16th, 1868 — The sleet that has been prevailing for several days has not entirely vanished, the earth seems as if covered with countless gems, look where you will and flakes of ice meet your eye at every turn. Cousin John was here a short while this afternoon. Lizzie is still with me, we intend to try our fortunes again tonight, perhaps we will be more successful. Let us try them as we may we can never know the changes in our lives until they actually occur. What a season for dreaming girlhood is. It is to be forever in expectancy of what is to occur, to sit and form visions of what the future is to bring and how often does it bring sorrow instead of joy, pain instead of pleasure. I often allow myself to grow sentimental, and at such times fondly do I turn to the past where commenced my first dreams of love, when earth looked bright and beautiful and my heart had known no shade to mar its sunshine, or even knew how to comprehend distrust, all I met was to me true and good, but years and close observation has taught me better, and driven out the belief that all are not true, who profess. Often as I gaze down through the past, how long seems the years that have fled since then. Oh how inexpressibly short are those years, when I first began to love and trust. It seems as if some short day flown almost in perceptibly on "downy feet" and those who first taught me did learn a heart lesson. How dear and how familiar their faces rise before me tenderly do they gaze with their truthful loving eyes into mine, and seem to say "Love me still." How then can I look upon this life's first youthful years with indifference? I cannot although I am still beloved. Yes! it is not vanity that prompts me to confess it, but it is sweet to know, would that I loved as ardently as others do. I may in course of time learn the same lesson contained in the past.

Friday, Jan 17th 1868 — Cold, very. Aunt Becca arrived today, was much pleased to see her. Sue came over after supper and staid an hour or so. Lizzie and I have had a considerable confab tonight, must hurry to bed as it is getting late.

Sunday, Jan 19th 1868 — Cousin John came this morning, made fire in the parlor after dinner, had quite a considerable chat with him. I am at a loss to comprehend an enigma is he in many respects, but doubly so in this cast. Late in the afternoon, S. and D. came, left soon after nightfall. How much I wished to warn him if there was danger, really I feel an interest deeper than I have known before. I would have every evil averted, every temptation overcome. His path should be a bright one while here, and after death, a blissful eternal rest.

Monday Jan 20th 1868 — A dull gloomy day, commenced teaching Georgie and Maggie today. Cousin John remained all night, had another conversation this evening. I cannot yet understand it. Alas! how deceptive is human nature. I reflect until I am lost in a perfect maze of doubt and then I turn with disgust. Surely I have an influence that I did not know I possess. It steals so imperceptibly that he will tell me all almost before he is aware of it, but I will never violate the trust he has reposed in me. I can—not obtain only the information he may choose to impart, as I must not speak of it to another. The letter puzzles me beyond expression. I must and will try to learn more about it if possible.

Tuesday Jan 21st 1868 — Have been exceedingly busy today making a dress for Mother. It has been a dull rainy day. Eddie came this morning and is here tonight. I wrote to Ginia and Sister, hope I may hear from them soon. It is time I had received a letter from Darling. I want to hear from her if I cannot see her. I believe she loves me truly, let me doubt others, but her I cannot.

Thursday Jan 23rd — Did not write any last night, have been very busy all day and tonight also. I feel so much happier when I have been usefully employed. My chief happiness consists in contributing to the comfort of those around me of those I love best on earth, my own beloved ones here, at my comfortable home, where my life flows on calmly, peacefully. Only when I see fondly cherished hopes of other years blighted, a feeling of sad regret comes over me and I feel a little discontent then, and I sigh to know, "deep in my heart is a grave," containing a love of other years. Mr. J. H. was here this morning just from Hampton. Cousin William was here also, played several tunes on the piano for him, but still will come a thought to mar all smiles, all charms a conversation may contain.

Friday Jan 24th 1868 —— A bright calm day after the severe rain storm of yesterday. Finished Mother's dress today, also a pair of drawers tonight, it took me only six hours to make them. Cousin John came this evening, did not stay long. I received two papers and a letter from Darling full of tenderness and love for me. Bless her heart, I wish I could see her, her truth I never doubt. I wish I was more confiding sometimes than I am but I see so much in different individuals I perhaps distrust where I should not.

Sunday Jan 26th 1868 — The day has passed in usual quiet. Uncle Frank and son ate dinner here. Sir John came this evening, and he's just left. Spent the evening very agreeably. He was exceedingly gay and chatty, just what I like. What is the use for us to grow selfish and sullen, over our little disappointments? It is for our own good that we should have shade as well as sunshine.

Monday Jan 27th 1868 — A rainy day, cut out a dress body for Mother, made considerable progress, hope to finish the body tomorrow. Often in glancing at my heart history I feel as if wandering in some bright land, until I find it is only a thing of the past, an oasis whose brightest flowers are withered and whose fountains have been drained.

Tuesday Jan 28th 1868 — Gloomy weather still, it is quite damp and cool tonight. Finished a pair of drawers tonight and after I put my work by, wrote a letter to Darling. Hope I may get a letter tomorrow. I feel quite chilly and must stop writing.

Wednesday Jan 29th 1868 — I am almost surprised at the date my journal bears, the month has passed away almost imperceptibly, truly time flies so very swiftly bearing us onward with it its never resting current, likewise our joys and sorrows, and age and cares creep upon us, and we grow old forgetful of the time when, and at last read the past like some large interesting volume, and it seems as if only a few short days or weeks has expired, when viewing life's first awakening. The hail has been pelting the window panes, and all probability it will be a stormy night. Have finished Mother's body, sewed on Maggie's dress and afterward made tatting and read.

Thursday Jan 30th 1868 — Extremely cold, the ground is covered with a slight snow, notwithstanding it is perfectly clear tonight and brightest stars are twinkling above. I hope it will soon moderate.

Friday Jan 31st 1868 — It has moderated exceedingly since yesterday and tonight it is truly beautiful, a night fit to inspire one with sentiment. Uncle Barnie and Alex ate dinner here. I feel so sorry for Mollie, her Mother seems so lowspirited. Poor girl, how sad she must feel to see her Mother thus. I should like so much to see her.

Saturday Feb 1st 1868 — Clear and beautiful. Nothing of importance has transpired today. Sent a letter to Darling today. Mrs. M. Patrick was here a short while this afternoon. I feel dull and sleepy. Received a letter from Cousin Levin this morning.

Sunday Feb 2nd 1868 — Mrs. Fletcher left for Hampton this morning after being weather bound almost two weeks. The first part of the day was damp and cloudy, but the afternoon was very bright. The day has been unusually quiet. No one has been here except Mr. Cook who ate dinner here which is quite unusual for the Sabbath. Lizzie is staying with Mrs. Hudgins. I hope she will soon come home, as I wish to know something definite concerning our proposed visit.

Monday Feb 3rd 1868 — Have been very busy all day braiding a yoke, did admirably, having more than half finished braiding it. Nothing of interest has transpired. The weather is exceedingly cold, and tonight the moon and hosts of stars are shining brightly upon the still cold earth, and many are the scenes it may shine on even at this moment, happy homes, joyous youth in its first fond dreams of love and coming bliss, and also more deplorable scenes, also abodes of vice and misery breaking hearts and all ills that fill up this life of ours. Such are the sins that make a sinful rebellious world.

Tuesday Feb 4th 1868 — Finished braiding my yoke today, it looks quite pretty. Wrote two letters tonight, one to Cousin Levin and the other to Mamie. Hope I may get a paper and a letter tomorrow. I have been thinking of writing a composition either prose or poetry. I sometimes feel quite poetical but cannot always frame my thoughts to the style I like. They are deep yet I cannot plunge down and bring from their depths gems to suit my fancy. The past contain all of my most precious heart gems, and it is there where I could only glean the finest, prettiest sentiments. The present seems too like a stern reality, knowing none of that beauty that the past contains. True, I am or try to be content, yet I labor under no elysian dream to at last find that reality must act its part. I, with all of woman's instinct know and feel the happiest days of my life have passed. Life's first awakening I think can never be like its wiser, elder moments. We then see so much to tell us that are not happier from knowing more of the world and its people. I write as if I am growing old. True, I am not old yet but will be some of these days if I live, perhaps I will look back to this period and think I was then "so happy."

Wednesday Feb 5th 1868 — Ah many are the memories that come crowding through my mind as I glance at the date my journal began. Just think today 6 years ago, it really does not seem so long, yet it is. I can scarcely realize it so swiftly, yet so sadly have those years flown. What an interesting period it was to me. I revert to it with many a sigh for years so bright and blest. It was then a pair of mournful expressive black eyes looked to me for love and sympathy. A lovely day it was and how surprised was I, to know that I was beloved by one so good, so noble, my heart beat responsive in sympathy to his own. I knew it was one of earth's most pearly gems that was laid at my feet, true proud noble wealth of heart love. I could not bear to cast it aside lightly. I was almost bewildered. I knew not what to do. I gave it up to God, to teach me what to do, and He took it all to himself and saved me the pain of wounding either, yet sent a grief more poignant. I knew both were gone, both that loved me so truly. I try to calmly look upon it. God alone knows what course I should have pursued. The shrine I had reared forgetful of its frailty was destined to be crushed ere I had learned to too soon and ardently worship the Idol. I hardly know my own self in regard to this subject. I cannot give the real impression. I wish I should have been compelled to a unison one way or the other. I could write pages, yet what would it avail, not one hour of the happy past can it restore, not one smile or word from the departed, the loved and lost. I know too much cannot be said in the praise of God's noblest work, free from the grosser defects that mankind generally. I must stop or I shall go on in this strain writing a short life History, until the night will be waning fast.

Thursday, Feb 6th 1868 —— Finished braiding my sleeves, and commenced embroidering. The weather has changed considerably since yesterday and now it looks lovely. The moon is shining brightly, and the sky is cloudless, a night fit for the Poet and ardent dreamer and lover of Nature. I love it as much and feel spellbound when gazing out as far as the eye can reach on its many little beams casting here and there a shadow. Kindly beams are they for they shine gratuitous on all the pure and holy, also the evil and unjust, and are the lonely vigil that keep watch over many a lone and distant grave of beloved ones far, far away.

Friday, Feb 7th 1868 —— Have been busy as usual all day, had a slight aching in my shoulder tonight which prevented me from work-

ing as late as usual. Hope I may receive a letter and papers
tomorrow. Lizzie has come home. I must go and see her as soon
as I can. Heard from Mollie this evening. I must write her the
next opportunity for I know she has a dull lonely time at best.
Wish I could see her.

Saturday Feb 8th 1868 — Wrote two letters this morning, did not
feel very well afterwards, consequently have not made myself
very busy the remainder of the day. I feel a little lazy tonight.
Sir John was here this evening but did not see his lordship, perhaps he came on business. Received no paper today, cannot
imagine why. I am really tired of waiting for them. Will now
read and prepare for bed, where I may be blessed with pleasant
dreams.

Sunday Feb 9th 1868 — An unusual quiet rainy day, had no company at all during the day. After my domestic duties were
performed, read Tennyson, and my Bible. Such a calm holy
Sabbath, a day to let our thoughts have more of Heaven than
earth. Yet the mind is uncontrollable and the thoughts that
come perhaps are not what they should be, free from all that
make our nature selfish, and too often do we find ourselves or
rather myself thinking too much of earth, its joys, some flown,
gone, gone forever. Often during this day has images of other
years filled my memory. Again I see the faces of those who
loved me in days of yore, and heart. I sometimes feel I would
not have it lo, it could not make me happier, for oh how sweet
yet sad is it to think over, and view again some familiar scene
with my mind's eye, to hear again with my imaginative ear true
words that had a power to thrill my inmost soul. The future
holds not one "bright particular star" for me. I may live long
and even contentedly, God only knows, but I feel the first bud
of love, its first young leaves are faded, withered. The brightest
star there has set. The clouds arose and brought a storm to
crush many a girlish as well as matron's heart, and 'tis not one
alone that has felt the shadow of sorrow and disappointment.
Our sunny land has them in many a household once so glad-
some.

Monday Feb 10th 1868 — Par left for Baltimore this morning. Cousin Howard went with him to Hampton. He brought me two papers and a letter from Sister. She is very well. Well, Sir John was here this morning. He was looking as smiling and happy as possible. Hope he is. He is noble hearted and deserves to be happy even if I cannot be instrumental, I can treat him with that sincere respect I feel for those who love me. Have been embroidering on my yoke today, and tonight have been reading in my papers.

Tuesday Feb 11th 1868 — Nature is wrapped in her winding sheet of beautiful snow. It is quite cold but the little stars are twinkling brightly, making our earth so lovely. Cousin John and Kit ate dinner here. He (Cousin John) did not leave until nearly night. Embroidering all day.

Wednesday Feb 12th 1868 — The ground is still covered with snow, Notwithstanding the fine weather, myriads of little lights bedeck the sky, and gives a lovely view as the eye glances upward and then downward, a contrast that man with all his skill is a mere nothing in producing so grand a scene. Have been embroidering during the day, read Tennyson and tonight made tatting.

Thursday Feb 13 1868 — The air has been mild and the snow disappeared rapidly. Embroidering again today. Sir John came here this afternoon, came into supper and did not leave until 11 o'clock P.M. Had quite a pleasant time, he was very loquacious and interesting. Par returned safe and well today.

Friday Feb 14th 1868 — Mother and Aunt Becca spent the day with Cousin Sarah. Eddie was here this morning. Mollie has returned to the Court House. I am glad she is back again. Many are the sentimental and comic flatteries have been going on today according to the usual custom. I expect some tomorrow as it is mail day. Went to Mrs. King's this evening. My hands are chapped so badly they really hurt me. Must prepare for bed.

Saturday Feb 15th 1868 — Received a paper today. Have not done anything of much importance. Made a little necktie for Mr. B. for a Philopena. Wish I could get a letter from Darling. Have received no valentines as yet.

Sunday Feb 16th 1868 — A nice day, almost like spring. Mr. Cooke and Uncle Barnie ate dinner here. Several gentlemen were here this evening, Mr. J. Hudgins, M. Hudgins, Dr. Bennett, Charlie and Kit. Charlie's horse got away, consequently he had to remain all night. Spent the evening tolerably pleasant. Cousin Martha left this evening for home.

Monday Feb 17th 1868 — Have been embroidering all day, and reading. Mrs. King was here this evening. I am so anxious to go and see Lizzie, hope I may get there this week. Ah it is saddening to think how much sin and misery make up this world. Oh my God protect and shield the innocent! I would live in virtue's holiest ways. I try to pursue the path of rectitude and duty. I heard today of a poor girl who has fallen from all that makes life desirable. Oh what must be her feelings, lonely, destitute, disgraced. Man, how often do you prove a serpent in "Eden's bower." Many a pure life thou hast blighted and left desolate. Yet woman still trusts too often to be deceived ere she will spurn you. You who should be her guide, her counselor to teach the way of truth, often proves her Nemesis in every joy.

Tuesday Feb 18th 1868 — Embroidering today as usual. The weather is bright and beautiful. Nothing of much interest has transpired. Sir John came here late this evening and Levin went home with him to attend a party. I expect they are enjoying themselves finely about now. Received a letter from Ginia Cooke today, will answer it soon. Hope I may get to see Lizzie sometime this week. I feel a little sleepy and dull, do not feel like writing at much length.

Friday Feb 21st 1868 — I have been to see Lizzie therefore have not written in my journal for several nights. Returned this morning, Lizzie came with me and is here tonight. Have finished my yoke and have been sewing on my chemise today.

Saturday Feb 22nd 1868 — A lovely day, made a pudding for dinner, made yeast and sewed a little on Mother's dress. So quickly has the day passed away, none would judge it to be the birthday of one of Virginia's noblest Sons, heard no firing of cannon. Nothing to remind one of the great Hero.

Sunday Feb 23rd 1868 — Attended to my domestic duties as usual this morning. No one called until the evening when **Mr. J. Hudgins** and **Mr. M. Hudgins** came. They remained until nine o'clock. The evening passed off quite pleasantly. Was very much amused at **Mr. M. Hudgins**. He commenced to relate a piece of gossip he heard relative to his being married, and became so very much confused could not proceed. I forgot to mention Gibie was here also and took supper with us. Lizzie left this evening, could not prevail on her to remain longer. Received a song from Sissie Mc_.

Monday Feb 24th 1868 — I awoke this morning and found the ground covered slightly with snow. It afterward snowed very fast and seemed to portend a deep snow but it is now raining and by the morning it will have disappeared. Finished Mother's dress and sewed sleeves in my chemise. I must make haste for the night is waning and I begin to feel cold. My yeast worked beautifully today and I have made up some light cake to rise by the morning.

Tuesday Feb 25th 1868 — My light cake was a failure. Have been very busy all day. Sewed on my chemise this evening. I feel dull, duller than I have for a long time.

Wednesday Feb 26th 1868 — A dull, misty, rainy day. Cousin John brought Ressie to Dr. King's. He came here and remained until after dinner, did not leave until nearly night. Commenced braiding a yoke today, also wrote a short note to Sister.

Thursday Feb 27th 1868 — The gloom of yesterday still prevails, and sunlight would be quite cheerful so closely has he kept himself all week. I hope it may soon clear off. I was dreaming nearly all night last night of **Mrs. Williams**. Have thought of her frequently during the day, and with her has come the memory of another, and often has his image presented itself during the day. All are useless, he cares not for my thoughts now, for a sainted life is his, and I am of this earth a frail being. Oh if friends that have gone before are guardian Angels. How beautiful the thought. Are they still permitted to cast one thought to those they loved on earth and do they still love, cheering indeed if true. I have fondly today viewed with my mind's eye

scenes of bygone joys, and yearned to recall them but alas! I
cannot bring to life not one petal of the roses that lie withered
in life's garden, or one smile that beamed so brightly.

Friday Feb 28th 1868 — Maggie and I went to Mrs. King's this morning, staid until dinner time, spent the morning very agreeably.
Have been braiding today on my yoke. Uncle Barnie was here
this evening. He says Mrs. Curtis is much worse. Oh how I do
pity her and sad indeed is her situation. Far better a last long
sleep in the quiet grave, where life's turmoil is ended. Mollie
too, how sad I feel for her. I know she must prefer death to
insanity for that Mother.

Saturday Feb 29th 1868 — A bright cold day. Received a paper and
two letters, one from Sister, the other from Cousin Levin. Made
pastry and cakes this morning. Ressie is here tonight, she came
yesterday. Must prepare to retire.

Sunday March 1st 1868 — The spring again is here, and ere long little flowers will be peeping from their lowly beds. Changes oh
many ere the winter will again appear. Many smiles will be
effaced by tears, and bright eyes lose their brightness, some in
death, some in sorrow. Great God thou alone can tell and guard
our destinies. Ressie went to Mrs. King's after breakfast but
returned to dinner. Victoria came with her. Cousin John took
dinner here also. Mr. Bennett was here to supper, left about 9
o'clock. The rain is pattering off the roof.

Monday Mar 2nd 1868 — A real spring morning, arose very early
and cooked breakfast. Aunt Louisa is sick. Commenced a sun
bonnet for myself this afternoon. I heard from Mollie today.
She is at Uncle Barnie's. Her Mother is much worse. Wrote her
a note by Alex. I feel right tired tonight as I have been on my
feet all day. Ressie was here this morning, staid only a few minutes.

Tuesday March 3rd 1868 — Cooked breakfast again this morning.
Aunt Louisa is better. She came in after breakfast and attended
as usual, to her work. Have been alone all day. Mother, Aunt
Becca and Maggie spent the day at Mrs. Cooke's, but I never
feel lonely when I am busy. Almost finished my bonnet. It is
extremely cold but the sky is cloudless. I think I never saw the

stars brighter. I noticed one particular, a star of the first magnitude it has such a brilliant light. I will not write at much length as I feel chilly.

Wed March 4th 1868 — Finished my sunbonnet soon after dinner and commenced braiding. Brother Willie came up with the mail. Was very anxious I should go back with him but the weather was so cold I did not go. Received a letter from Mollie this morning. I know she must feel oh so unhappy! And to add to her sorrow, some will tattle and say things she never thought of. Wrote a letter to Sister and sent the tatting. Victoria, Veddie and Granville came over tonight. I went to Mrs. King's this evening and Ressie came back with me. She is here tonight. Cousin John was here this morning. It is very cold tonight and perfectly clear.

Thursday March 5th 1868 — Braided on my yoke this morning and read all the afternoon. I was at Mrs. King's a short while this evening. Levin carried Ressie home late this afternoon. Mrs. Curtis was to be carried to the Asylum today. I wonder if she went. How horrible it must be for Mollie to see her only Parent so affected. None can tell her feelings of anguish, but that all omnipresent Being who sees and knows every woe, may He in his mercy be with her in her hours of loneliness and comfort her young heart so soon learned this is a world of sorrow, amounting almost to despair. Have not heard from Darling for four long weeks. I cannot imagine why she does not write. I fear she is sick.

Friday March 6th 1868 — Finished braiding my yoke and nearly finished stitching it. Had the kitchen room upstairs scoured out as I expect to teach school Monday. Heard from Sister today, she is tolerably well. Sir John came by from Hampton and ate supper with us. He brought me a letter from Mrs. Stores. She seems very anxious about Sister, how I wish it was over. I feel oh so very, very anxious myself. I must go to Hampton as soon as I can to see them. I want to see her oh so much.

Saturday March 7th 1868 — Wrote four letters this morning. It has been a real spring day. Mended a little this evening. Sir John came in and made an engagement to take me to church tomorrow if the weather is propitious. I almost wish I had not made the engagement, as I fear it may be some trouble and his horse is not in a very good condition for traveling. Received my paper this morning.

Sunday March 8th 1868 — Unusually warm. The air was warm and balmy consequently enjoyed my ride to church exceedingly. Saw Mr. Bennett and Mr. Malcolm. He was looking exceedingly well. Billie Wood, Mr. Patrick and Mr. J. Hudgins ate dinner here. After dinner Mr. Bennett and Mr. M. Hudgins came. Have enjoyed myself so much today! Cousin John came late this afternoon and ate supper with us. Par has been complaining all day. Mother went this afternoon to see Uncle Kit. Tomorrow I commence my school duties, Providence permitting.

Monday March 9th 1868 — Have been doing very little of anything this beautiful spring day. Aunt Becca, Victoria and I walked to see Uncle Kit remained until after supper. Mr. Hogg came while we were there and walked home with us. Oh, what a lovely night it is! And how the mind on such a night filled with inspiration, feels a depth of calm which no other time has power to cast such a sweet yet saddening influence, and inspires one with real sentiment. Earth's many vices are for the time forgotten, and all around seems pure and true. The very air seems to speak purity and the little golden beams and twinkling stars keeping lonely vigils through the night speak to us of the Wisdom and Goodness of the God who made them. Sir John and Eddie ate supper here. I did not see them as I remained upstairs while they were at supper.

Tuesday March 10th 1868 — Mother and Par left early this morning for Hampton. It has been a delightful day. They returned about twilight. Sister is quite well and Mrs. Stores. I am glad to hear from them. Cousin John ate dinner with us. Victoria was here this morning. Cousin William was here this afternoon. Have been braiding on my sleeves. The spring weather has a tendency to make me feel dull.

Wednesday March 11th 1868 — The day has passed as usual, finished one of my sleeves and commenced another. Went to Mrs. King's this afternoon. It is much cooler tonight than it has been for many nights. Have been cutting bed quilt pieces since supper. Today was the birthday of one of my dear friends, had he lived to see it, but he like the brave and true lost his life on the far off battle plain, and tonight he quietly sleeps free from earth's cares and sorrows. I know his rest is blissful for he was good and true, and the little stars are the lone watchers that twinkle tonight upon his silent grave. Who can tell what would have been the result had he lived. Now no fears disturb his breast, and oh, if the departed are permitted to think of those who dwell on earth, does he tonight think of those who loved, and gaze upon them from his home above? Ah none can dare answer the question but if so, blessed thought, to think we are still beloved by the sainted dead.

> *"What are a thousand living loves*
> *To those that cannot quiet the dead."*

Thursday March 12th 1868 —— When I awoke this morning the first sound that greeted my ear was the pattering of rain which has been incessant until about twilight. Have been braiding my sleeve and doubtless would have finished had I not stopped to wind some cotton. After supper cut bed quilt pieces. I feel rather dull, not inclined to write much. Will therefore stop just here and prepare for bed.

Friday March 13th 1868 —— Finished braiding my sleeve, and made two neck bows, one as a birthday present for Levin and the other for a dear friend. Wonder if he will appreciate it? I cannot help but like him. I composed, wrote some verses on Levin's birthday which is tomorrow. Afterwards pieced on my quilt. Par went to Hampton this morning. The rain ceased last night and it has been mild but chilly all day. Cousin John and Cousin Howard ate dinner here. Cousin John left about sunset. Cousin Howard is here now.

Saturday March 14th 1868 —— Received a letter and a paper. The letter was from Mr. T. M. Harwood. Although unacquainted, he wrote confiding Mollie, letter enclosed to my care. Wish I could see an opportunity to send it. Maggie broke Mollie's letter open thinking it was mine, and had a hearty cry about it. I have been darning all day. It has been cloudy and rained a little late this evening. If I can see my way will write to Mollie tomorrow. I wish I could see her. I know she is sad and lonely in her first great sorrow. Oh my God look with an all merciful eye upon her and give her that comfort and peace "that passeth all understanding." If this earth contained the limit of all our hopes, our fears, and our loves, we would indeed be a people whose destiny would be despicable, but there is a better world beyond where love, hope and joy are immortal, and where earth's weary pilgrims may have a rest eternal, and where no adverse storms blight the buds of hope or steal those we love most and best.

Sunday March 15th 1868 —— Wrote to Mollie this morning and sent the letter by Mr. Hudgins. He invited me to take a ride with him, but I did not wish to make him wait and I was not ready to go. Had quite a pleasant chat with him, he was looking very lively. Cousin Mary Vaughn and her three children spent the day with us. Dr. Bennet and Gibie came this afternoon. Victoria came over also. Mr. Bennet left about twilight, Gibie remained all night. Mr. Hudgins came back to supper and brought Eddie with him.

Monday March 16, 1868 — Arose very early this morning to attend to some domestic arrangements, cut out a chemise after breakfast and almost made the body. Eddie came back this morning and told my fortune for me with cards. Cousin Sidney took supper with us and remains all night. Read Tupper a short while this afternoon.

Tuesday March 17th 1868 — Arose early this morning and cooked breakfast. Aunt Louisa was sick. Cooked dinner also, sewed a little on my chemise. Read Tupper a short while this afternoon. I try to employ my time usefully. If I fail, it is no fault of mine. Nothing of much interest has transpired. I feel as if I must try to write something before long.

Wednesday March 18th 1868 — My birthday. 23 years has swiftly fled with its lights and shadows leaving in their course sad experience, and few heart sorrows, connected with all are pleasant and happy reminiscences of my early girlhood, "days that knew no shade or sorrow." Many may think me happy as I so bravely wear the mask of calm content. Yet none know how deep in my heart is a grave where earth's first flowerets of love lie withered, its hope, its aspirations rudely swept by the storms of maturer years. Years that have stolen the fresh young thoughts and changed the trusting gay girl into a determined woman, teaching me the stern reality. Will the flowers of love and hope bloom again is a question I often ask myself, but cannot satisfactorily answer. Time alone will tell. God knows what joy or sorrow the future may bring. Of one thing I am sure, it can bring no joy dearer or brighter relative to earth than those the past contains, that past where first I knew to be loved, and love again. True, there are those left who love me now, I believe truly sincerely. Yet comes not the kindred feeling of days of yore. I feel a strange compassion for some, for others indifference. Gladly would I bestow the remnant of my heart's affection, but it is not at my will. The second awakening must be if to be there is spontaneous as the first. I cannot chain my heart or rule my destiny, a power infinite and unseen must perform the task. I could write pages but must soon stop. I wonder if I live how I will feel next birthday, if I will be glideing down the same monotonous stream, which has known no changes for sometime, and which perchance may always be as now.

Received a letter from Jennie and one from Sister, both are well. Sir John took dinner with us. He is as gay as usual. Wrote a short note to Sister and almost finished my chemise.

Thursday March 19th 1868 — Finished my chemise and commenced some crochet trimming. The day has been one of unusual beauty. Mother, Par and Maggie went to Mrs. Denton's. Mrs. Presson called in a short while this evening to engage her son to me for a scholar. Have not commenced teaching yet.

Friday March 20th 1868 — It has been a cloudy cold day. The rain has been incessant all the afternoon and tonight it is snowing very fast. I wrote a short composition this morning, will try to correct it tomorrow, and if it suits my fancy, will make an attempt to have it published. Crocheted a greater part of the day. Mr. Cook and Mr. Davis took dinner here. Aunt Becca has been indisposed all day.

Saturday March 21st 1868 —— Found the ground covered with snow this morning as soon as I awoke, but it has melted very rapidly and tonight there is very little remaining. Did not receive my paper as usual this morning, consequently was much disappointed. Wrote a letter to Jennie S. this morning. Sir John was here this evening, he was just from Hampton. Sister was well. He said he had a letter for me at his home. I hope he will come tomorrow and bring it. Cousin Howard took supper here as usual and remained all night. Have been mending my drawers, have just finished them before I commenced writing. Must hurry to bed for it is growing late and I feel chilly.

Sunday March 22nd 1868 —— A bright cold morning. Sir John and Dr. Bennett were here a short while this afternoon. Sir John brought my letter, it was from Darling. I was much pleased to hear from her. I don't like the strain much in which it is written, and fear she is not content. The letter left a gloomy feeling and have felt rather sad since.

Monday March 23rd 1868 —— Commenced a bosom for Par and crocheted a little. Veddie went to Hampton this morning, heard from Sister by him, she was very well. Received my paper and have been deeply absorbed in reading since supper. I met with a heart revelation in there, in some points coinciding with my own feelings so nearly I could not but feel how similar to myself. Ah! many are the sad heart histories, so many that none know, the volumes of anguish that have chased the glad sunshine of love and hope from girlish hearts, ere youth had fled, some by death and numbers by some rash act or look which we would barter the wealth of worlds to reclaim again those hours when revenge was sweeter than the nectar of the Gods, but its fruits more bitter than the "Apples of Sodom." Victoria was here a short while this morning. She brought me a book to read called the "Wandering Guerilla." Cousin Sarah was here a short time this afternoon. Mother went to Uncle Frank's to get some rose bushes.

Tuesday March 24th 1868 —— Have done nothing of much consequence during the day. Cousin Georgia and her husband came about 1 o'clock. He left about half past three P.M. She is going to remain several days with us. Have read a little in Victoria's paper. I feel very, very dull and sleepy.

Thursday March 26th 1868 — Left my ink downstairs consequently did not write last night as usual. Made another bosom for Par, finished it this evening. Have been very pleasantly engaged in conversation with Cousin Georgia. She has been relating some interesting anecdotes relative to the days of our young Confederacy. I sigh for those times when we were so happily situated but can only look back to it as the thirsty traveller sighs ever so sadly for some Oasis over which his weary feet have trod. A Wise Providence veiled the future, and we lived only in the enjoyment of the Present, little knowing the path our then untried feet must tread. Received a letter from Darling this afternoon. Must write by the next mail.

Friday March 27th 1868 — A dull rainy day. Nearly completed one of Par's shirts. Nothing of interest has transpired during the day. Do not feel much like writing, will therefore read and prepare for bed. Maggie sleeps with me now and she is undressed ready for bed.

Saturday March 28th 1868 — Wrote two letters this morning, one to Emily, the other to Darling. I wrote Emily quite a long letter, scolding but at the same time in an affectionate manner, for her neglect. I cannot tell why she should treat my letters with indifference. Never mind this is the last I shall write unless she answers it. I feel I have done my duty even more. I never thought our friendship was to last only a few years, but thought it for a lifetime. Tis thus all through life, friends forget the cares of the world come between the loves of earth, and one who professes to be a friend today, tomorrow may be a foe. Cousin William was here this morning and came back this afternoon. I played one tune for him, Cousin Georgia played several. I felt as if my very soul went out with some of the tunes she played and felt how much of the love of the beautiful my soul contained, sentiments worth more to me than gold, thoughts of my own heart experience. Made pies and custards this afternoon for dinner tomorrow.

Monday, March 30th 1868 — Staid down stairs so late last night, consequently did not write. Have finished one of Par's shirts. Cousin William was here this morning. Cousin Frances and Mary came yesterday, was very glad to see them. Par went to Hampton today, and brought my paper.

Tuesday March 31st 1868 — The stormy weather that has been prevailing for several days cleared away this morning. I sat upstairs all the morning waiting to see the bridal party pass, Miss Wynne and Mr. Howard. Cousin Frances, Georgie and Aunt Becca went to Cousin Sarah's. They remain all night. Have been sewing on Par's shirts and reading tonight.

Wednesday April 1st 1868 — Thoughts of beautiful bright days with flowers of beauty rise in the imagination at the word (April). This has been one of those beauteous days. Cousin Lizzie Wood and Hannah spent the day with us. Cousin William was here this morning. Cousin Frances and Cousin Georgia returned this evening. Have not done anything like sewing much today.

Thursday April 2nd 1868 — Have been sewing as usual, nothing of much interest has transpired. Have felt exceedingly dull as I was awake a greater part of the night with little Mary, who was sick. Lizzie and Victoria were over a short while this evening. Mrs. King came over after supper, staid until 9 o'clock.

Friday April 3rd 1868 — Par went to Hampton this morning, did not bring any letter for me. It has been damp and cloudy all day. Nothing of unusual interest has transpired. Finished Par's shirt.

Saturday April 4th 1868 — A bright day. Mended a greater part of the day. Cousin William and Mr. Patrick were here this morning. Dr. McLaughlin came late this afternoon. He remains all night.

Sunday April 5th 1868 — A bright cool day. Cousin Frances and Mary left this morning for Hampton. I was very busy all the morning preparing dinner. Cousin John ate dinner here. Cousin Georgia and Dr— left this afternoon. Mr. Hudgins and Dr. Bennet came this evening. Mr. Hudgins remained all night to go with Par to Norfolk. I thought Cousin John would never leave, He remained until after 10 PM.

Monday April 6th 1868 — Par and Mr. Hudgins left early this morning for Norfolk. Have been busy all day making a shirt for Levin, sewed as long as I could see. Par returned tonight, and expects to go to Hampton again tomorrow. Perhaps I may go too.

Monday April 13th 1868 — A week has elapsed since I last wrote. Have been to Hampton, staid from Wednesday until Sunday. Sister came home with me, brother Willie brought us. Have not been doing much. Crocheted a little trimming for a little shirt. Brother Willie returned today.

Sunday May 3rd 1868 — Aunt Becca and I anticipated going to church but was disappointed. It has been damp all the forenoon but the sun sunk brightly, calmly into the West. Uncle Barnie, Laura and children spent the day with us. Maggie still sick. Mrs. King (Sr.) was here this morning and evening. Howard V—, Cousin John and Uncle Frank ate dinner here. Mr. H—, Dr. B were here this evening. Cousin John, Dr. B— left about eight, Mr. H— about 9 o'clock P.M. Mr. Cooke ate supper.

Monday May 4th 1868 — Cloudy, cool day, a day of gloom without and within. I have felt anxious, troubled about my Darling precious little Maggie. I feel oh! so very uneasy about her for she is ill very. Oh my God! be merciful to us, in this our present need. Spare our little cherub to us a little longer, and if we sin in this request, forgive, for we are weak erring creatures. Why is it, I wonder, we shrink from death, from giving our best beloved to its embrace, when it is a valley all of us must pass through. If we are righteous it but leads to our Father's throne, and to a reunion to the loved and lost of other years. Granville commenced school today. Mrs. Cooke, Lizzie and Mrs. Dunton was here this morning, Mrs. King this evening. Mr. H— Vaughn worked here today and remains all night. Victoria came over tonight.

Wednesday May 6th 1868 — Did not write in my journal last night, had the headache so very badly. Have been up waiting on

Maggie last night, consequently feel a little dull. I am oh so thankful! that she seems better. Received a note from Brother Willie, Sister was much better. Sewed and finished a night gown shirt. Martha Presson and Cousin John were here this afternoon.

Thursday May 7th 1868 — A dull misty morn. Did not have but two pupils today, consequently dismissed school at dinner. I have felt dull. Maggie has been exceedingly restless all day. A severe storm of wind and rain arose this afternoon. I have done nothing of much importance. Read right much this afternoon. Victoria was here a short while.

Friday May 8th 1868 — Cloudy — very cool tonight, school. Commenced braiding on Aunt Becca's sleeves. Maggie seems better than she has done since her sickness. Read a little since supper. Georgie is very unwell tonight. I bathed his feet, rubbed his breast in mustard — hope by the morning he will be much better. Must hurry to bed, it is growing late. Mrs. Dunton was here this afternoon. Victoria was here tonight.

Saturday May 9th 1868 — Bright and cool. Maggie is better. Have done no sewing at all during the day. Wrote a sketch off entitled (In The Twilight). I intend finishing it and attempt to have it published. I hope it may meet with approbation. Read a part of the day in my papers. Victoria was here this afternoon. Her Cousin came (Mr. King) from Norfolk, she did not remain long after she knew he had come. Received a letter from Sister, she is up again. Oh! how thankful I am she is better.

Sunday May 10th 1868 — A day so lovely! fit to muse on all sacred and pure things, a beautiful day for church. Maggie is about the same as yesterday. Victoria and her Cousin came over this afternoon. Dr. Bennett and Sir John were here also. Mr. Bennet left about sunset. Sir John left a little later, told us goodbye, but he had not been gone very long before he came back, remained until 9 P.M. He was very gay, amused Aunt Becca and I, and drew my photograph on the wall.

Monday May 11th 1868 — Cloudy and rainy. Did not have but two pupils today, the weather being so inclement. Sewed on my nightgown this afternoon, braided on Aunt Becca's sleeve in school. Maggie better. Victoria and Mr. King were here this afternoon. The evening passed off very pleasantly. I told their fortunes. Levin went to Mr. Phillips's this afternoon. Par was very much worried as he wants his horse to plow.

Tuesday May 12th 1868 — I can hardly realize the month is so far advanced. All of my pupils except my little Darling and Georgie were present. Have done no sewing whatever. I am so very sleepy I must stop. Mrs. Dunton was here this morning.

Wednesday May 13th 1868 — The rain poured in torrents. I had only one pupil to come. Sent him home again as the weather was so inclement. Maggie did not seem so well this morning but appears better tonight. Received a letter in the mail this morning from Emily. I was very glad to hear from her, have thought so much about her today. She, I don't think ought to be surprised at the reception of my letter. She speaks of coming soon. I hope she may, although it will recall Oh! so much in the past to see her. I know I shall feel sad. We have never met since we parted seven years ago, long and dreary years. Many are the changes since then. Neither of our lives had known one shade of sorrow, when we spoke the goodbye, and little did we know the shadows that were then gathering in our sky. The War had actually commenced, but none of its direful effects were felt. There were no graves enclosing the forms of the loved ones we possessed. All was one day of joy and sunshine to our hopeful youthful hearts. It will seem like that dear old time in some respects to see her, but few very few, those were with us, or connected, where are they? Some dead, some estranged, and some married. Wrote two letters, one to Jennie S— and one to Harry Harbert, Esq.

Thursday May 14th — A day of bright sunshine, everything looked lovely as far as the eye could reach. I went out this morning early, and as I gazed up at the blue sky and beautiful green trees, putting forth their leaves so fresh, heard the birds warbling their Matin songs, I thought it enough to make the soul forget its realities of sorrows and toils. I thought how lovely! was God's handiwork, how infinitely small were our best and noblest deeds in comparison. All things seem to rejoice, the

most minute flower adds a charm to Nature. They seem as if
sent to beautify our earth and cheer the heart of man. They
bloom and cast their fragrance over graves where are sleeping
the bravest and best, the purest and loveliest of our land.
Thank God our little darling seems better. Mr. Hudgins went to
Hampton today, brought me a letter from Sister. She is doing
very well. Victoria was here a short time this morning. Mr. H——
ate supper here.

Friday May 15th 1868 — Sunshine and clouds. Braided on Aunt
Becca's sleeve during school hours, did nothing else afterward.
Pattie Wade spent the afternoon here. Cousin Howard went for
her and went back with her. I believe he is courting her
notwith——standing his assertions to the contrary. My little
Precious seems very feeble and weak. God grant she may soon
be restored to us, for I am oh so anxious! Mrs. King and little
Cecil Powell were here this evening.

Saturday May 16th 1868 — Another bright day. Mended my dress,
and went over to Mrs. King's this afternoon to call on Miss
Marion and Sadie, staid about two hours. Thank God Maggie
seems better today. Wrote two letters this morning, one to
Mamie and the other to Sister. I feel dull and sleepy, will read
and prepare for bed.

Sunday May 17th 1868 — Pouring rain all the morning and a greater
part of the afternoon. The sun afterwards came out in his
splendor making all nature appear lovely. Maggie is better, ate
more than usual today. Mr. Hudgins was here tonight. I don't
think he was as gay as he usually is, something troubles him
perhaps. Levin went to Uncle Kit's this evening after supper.

Monday May 18th 1868 — Bright and cool. Nothing of unusual interest transpired during the day. Made two cakes this evening, one
a sponge, the other a butter cake. Sat up with Maggie a greater
part of last night, consequently feel very dull.

Tuesday May 19th 1868 — Today the counterpart of yesterday.
Maggie is better. I am so glad she is improveing. Received a
letter from Sister and a short note from Mrs. Stores. Wish I
would hear from Darling. I am so sleepy. Finished one of Aunt
Becca's sleeves, commenced my night gown sleeves.

Wednesday May 20th 1868 —— It does not really seem like the month of flowers, the air is so damp and cold. Have done nothing of any consequence except my school duties. Brother Willie came today. I was very glad to see him. Sister is getting along finely. Maggie is improveing also. Truly am I thankful for such blessings. Received my paper today. Cousin William was here this morning, remained sometime, played a tune on the piano.

Thursday May 21st 1868 — A day bright, cool. Braided on Aunt Becca's other sleeve in school, Did scarcely nothing afterward. Miss Marion, Sadie, and Mrs. Cooke and Lizzie spent the evening here. Miss Marion and Sadie remained until nearly 10 P.M., enjoyed myself right much. Cousin William was here this morning and afternoon also. He was very chatty. Maggie is getting along more than we could expect.

Friday May 22nd 1868 — The morning very pretty and pleasant. About dinner the sky became clouded, and all the afternoon has been showery. Made my nightgown sleeves after school. Nothing of interest has transpired, nothing to dispel the monotony prevailing. I feel dull, dull, and will be very brief.

Saturday May 23rd 1868 —— A gloomy day, showery as March or April. Received a letter from Darling this morning, she speaks of wishing to come with a view to teaching. I hope she may come. Johnnie Phillips ate supper here, and remains all night. Wrote to Emily this morning, I expect soon to hear from her and to hear she is coming. Maggie is improving very much. Hope we may go to church tomorrow.

Sunday May 24th 1868 — The morning damp, cloudy and clear alternately. Mr. Bennet came and carried Aunt Becca and I to the brick Church. I enjoyed it very much. Dr. Bullard preached for us, and a very good sermon. We arrived home about 1/2 past 2 P.M. Found Cousin Martha here and one of My friends. Ah who can tell! what a day may bring forth. Mr. Bennet and Sir John left here about sunset, another gentleman did not leave until after 12 o'clock P.M. I thought he would get tired of talking to me. He made an open declaration which I hardly expected. We conversed freely, I keeping my way smooth, never giving him any room to say what he so much desired. He had to come to the point unaided. I would not assist him but he was determined that I should know all. I thought him cold and inflexible but how I was mistaken. He is affectionate and warm hearted with those whom he loves. How much I wished to say I omitted, could not think of until now, perhaps I may never have an opportunity of doing so again. I believe he loves me yet there is a mystery attending all of the past I cannot solve. It surprised, astonished me when he just mentioned the subject last summer. I thought perhaps the dream was by this time dispelled. I feel sorry such is the case. I must have an explicit chat. Why could I not tell him, all reasons will comfort him, but something deemed to urge me to act a little contrary, which he said I was, and seemed determined I should come to a definite decision but I did not. He was perplexed, bothered "knew not what to make of me," he said. I know not what to think of him, both are enigmas one to the other.

Monday May 25th 1868 — Clear bright day. Made some crochet braid trimming for Mother. Maggie has had her clothes on all day, is looking much better. I have been dull all day. I sat up so late last night, I have come back in my room to sleep tonight. I feel like I am right again.

Tuesday May 26th 1868 —— Beautiful and cool this morning, finished my crochet trimming. Lizzie was here this afternoon, she and Sallie remained until after supper. Ah me, I sigh, I know not why! I gaze out, the beautiful firmament is studded with stars, one bright particular "star of the evening." To gaze upon it is to inspire one with thought of Heaven, love and truth. There is no bright star on which my soul gazes. I wish I had not learned to know how fleeting is all earthly love. Who can tell those who are really true? I should not talk so as I who have never been deceived, but blessed with the true. So far so good. I may yet be deceived, if so woe to the deceiver, who will strike out every feeling of confidence in the whole race of men.

Wednesday May 27th 1868 —— Only think! I have paid two visits this afternoon, it seems really strange! so little I go out. Taught school as usual. After school went to see Lizzie, remained until after supper. Mrs. Smith and Martha Presson were there, they came home as we did. Went to Mrs. King's after I came back, staid until after 9 o'clock.

Thursday May 28th 1868 — Had a very severe rainstorm before the day broke this morning which made the air very pleasant. Commenced repairing my light dresses. Mr. Patrick came today to do brick work. Miss Marion, Sadie and Cecil were here tonight.

Friday May 29th 1868 — Clear and cloudy alternately. A shower came on about two but did not last long. Fixed one of my summer dresses after school.

Saturday May 30th 1868 — Very cloudy and damp. Mr. Bennet came up this morning to accompany the young Ladies from Mrs. King's to Hampton. He came to the door and talked to me a short time. Mr. Tilford came also and brought me a letter from Mollie. Victoria, Cecil and Granville were here tonight. Aunt Becca and I expect to go to church tomorrow if the weather is propitious. I hope it may. Cousin Nancy Wade was here this morning and gives glowing accounts of the meeting.

Sunday May 31st 1868 — A beautiful Sabbath, went to church as anticipated. Troy carried Aunt Becca and I. The congregation was immense. Had a splendid discourse from Dr. Bullard on the Unity of Christ. Came home to dinner, found Cousin Mary and the children here and Mr. Vaughn. They left about five P.M. Mr. Hudgins, Cousin John and Dr. Bennet and Mr. R. Cooke came also. Cousin John and Mr. Cooke left about twilight after making an engagement to carry us to Church tomorrow night. Mr. Bennet left just before dark, Mr. Hudgins about 9 P.M. Cousin Howard and Mr. Hudgins in their mischief made me walk down the road a little way just to tease me.

Monday June 1st 1868 — Summer is here or at least the summer month. June seems to tell us of dreamings, in the first dawn of Nature's bright beautiful days, the flowers bright, the trees luxuriant in their foliage, all speak of the Great God who made them subservient to our comfort and happiness. Laura and Uncle Barnie and children spent the day here. I am so glad we can go to church tonight.

Tuesday June 2nd 1868 — An exceedingly bright morning. Aunt
Becca and I went to church as anticipated, had a very pleasant
ride and enjoyed the meeting. Dr. Bennet carried Aunt Becca
instead of Mr. Cooke. I planned the excursion. I was particu-
larly desirous she should go. We left here after sunset and Mr.
Cooke came after we left and those who staid behind told us
he was very angry because he was disappointed. All here have
been teazing Aunt Becca about fooling him, but we will make it
all right. Cousin John's curiosity was unbounded yesterday relative to my journal. I brought it down to show him a piece in
there about the Picnic. He was not satisfied with that but
wished to read a piece he found relative to our last Summer's
conversation. I am very sorry he read it. I did not wish him to
know he was so explicitly understood. He thinks strange of my
manner, my indecision and I think him mysterious, wonderful
in many respects.

Wednesday June 3rd 1868 — Very unlike June, cloudy and cool.
Taught as usual, sewed on Maggie's baby dress, wrote a note
to Sister. Aunt Becca has been sick all day. Will stop writing
as it is growing late.

Thursday June the 4th 1868 — Very cloudy all day. Sewed on Maggie's
baby dress. Mrs. King senior was here this afternoon. Victoria
and Miss Marion left today for Williamsburg. Cousin Martha
went to Uncle Frank's this morning. Nothing of interest has
transpired. The workmen are still here building. Our little
Maggie, thank God is progressing rapidly.

Friday June 5th 1868 — Cloudy like yesterday. Sewed again on
Maggie's dress. After school Aunt Becca and I made 41 cakes
for the Store. Cousin John ate dinner here. I must really write
my MS. and send it for publication, if it meets with sufficient
approbation. I feel right tired, after my fatigue. Whenever
there comes a thought of the loved and lost ones, I think them
oh with so much purity! to think they are so good and true,
forever blessed, "forever with the Lord."

Saturday June 6th 1868 — Clear and bright this morning. Wrote this
morning indeed until nearly dinner, felt very dull afterward,

did nothing of much importance. Mr. and Mrs. Davis were here a short time this afternoon.

Sunday June 7th 1868 —— More cloudy than otherwise. Par and Cousin Howard went to Uncle Barnie's, Mr. Bennett came in a short while this morning on his way to church. After dinner Cousin William, Mr. Bennett and Gibie were here. Mr. Bennett came here from Church. We had all been to dinner when he came. It was long time before I could prevail on him to have a snack. Aunt Becca and I went in the cookroom and fixed dinner for him. Cousin William came in with him. We sat there some time chatting, passing the time pleasantly. Both of them tried to teaze me. Sir John did not come at all. How he tries to impress me how he is perfectly callous to the past, better for him if he was.

Monday June 8th 1868 —— Several of my pupils were absent today. Crocheted during school hours, commenced repairing one of my dresses. I have such little time to sew, my time is so entirely engrossed with my school and domestic duties. I must write to Darling in a few days.

Tuesday June 9th 1868 —— Clear during the forenoon but the rain poured in torrents this afternoon. Finished repairing my dress, and commenced fixing another. Wrote to Darling tonight.

Wednesday June 10th 1868 —— The 7th anniversary of our famous "Bethel battle." It has been an incessant rain ever since the latter part of the morning. My finger feels very sore, consequently do not feel like writing.

Thursday June 11th 1868 —— Another rainy day. Repaired one of my dresses and commenced a lawn dress for myself. Aunt Becca is making the skirt for me, hope to finish it this week. Nothing unusual has transpired. I did not teach school, the weather was too inclement for any of the children to come.

Friday June 12th 1868 —— The rain has ceased, the day has been lovely. Made ruffles for my sleeves. Mr. Cooke sent the cart for us and we spent the evening there. Mr. Gibbs was there from Norfolk. Lizzie and I staid up stairs all the afternoon talking. Had only three pupils, consequently dismissed earlier.

Saturday June 13th 1868 — A day bright and pleasant. After going through the routine of my domestic duties, sewed on my lawn dress. Aunt Becca finished the skirt for me today. After dinner, Aunt and I made a cake for tomorrow's dinner. It will be Maggie's birthday. Alex Tabb ate dinner here today. My finger is much better than it has been. The sky is studded with stars. Among them is one star bright and beautiful. Shine on bright star, those are kindly beams you shed over the silent lone graves of so many of the young and gifted of our land. Though the kindest may forget. Yet constantly you linger, oh so softly above them. Have not seen S— for two weeks. Wonder when they will come again. It matters not.

Sunday June 14th 1868 — A beautiful Sabbath. Made boiled custard for dinner. Mr. Bennett came by and asked me to go to church. I was so much heated over the stove, Mother did not think it prudent for me to go. In the afternoon Cousin John, Mr. Hudgins and the Old Boss (alias Mr. Anderson) were here, also Cousin John ate supper here. Mr. Bennett left before supper. Mr. Hudgins and Cousin John remained until after 11 o'clock P.M. Enjoyed the evening right much.

Monday June 15th 1868 — Mrs. Sue Turner spent the day with us. She, her little boy and Sister, Cousin Martha left for Williamsburg. Crocheted a little today. Nothing of interest has transpired. My little Darling commenced school today.

Tuesday June 16th 1868 — A real summer day, taught as usual. Cousin Sarah came this afternoon and Aunt Becca went home with her. Miss her very much. Maggie sleeps with me tonight. Patsy was here this evening. Lizzie and Sallie were here also. Received two letters this evening from Sue and Ginia.

Wednesday June 17th 1868 — Very warm and a little sultry, had quite a rainstorm this afternoon. Cousin William was here this morning. Sewed on my dress body after school. I feel sleepy and weary, did not sleep well last night. Must hurry to bed.

Thursday June 18th 1868 — The rain of yesterday made the ground exceedingly wet. Crocheted during school. After school sewed on my dress body, and while waiting for Par to come to supper, read History. I have suddenly lost all interest in light literature. My mind craves something deeper. Levin left this afternoon for Fox Hill. Nothing of unusual interest has transpired.

Friday June 19th 1868 — Excessively warm. Sewed very little today. Mr. Anderson dined here today and remains all night. Just as we were about eating supper, Major Putnam and another Yankee stopped for supper and lodgings. I had to hurry and fix beds for them.

Saturday June 20th 1868 — After going through my usual routine of dusting and cleaning, sat down to my sewing and finished my dress. Received a note from Sister this morning inviting me to a Picnic. I am very anxious to go. Aunt Sarah and Uncle Frank spent the afternoon with us. Alex ate dinner and supper here also.

Sunday June 28th 1868 — More than a week has elapsed since I last wrote in this, during which time I have been in Hampton; went to the Picnic and enjoyed myself very much. Went to Hospital Point on the Portsmouth side, walked about the grounds, and through the Hospital, everything there is so convenient, so nicely arranged. Came back to Hampton about 7 P.M. Arrived at home to dinner today. Brother Willie and Sister came with me. I really love to be with Mrs. Stores. She is so kind to me, seems to wish all good for my welfare. I am sensitive and feel an interest in those who care for me, feel grateful beyond measure. Sir John was here this evening.

Monday June 29th 1868 — Arose early this morning and commenced my usual school and domestic duties. Sister went home this afternoon. Lizzie, Sallie Griffin and Sallie Cook and Bettie Smith were here, also old Mrs. King. I felt sad and depressed tonight. What avail is it to be impetuous? It only increases our cares and toils. I try not to be too impulsive.

Tuesday June 30th 1868 — When I awoke this morning it was very cloudy and soon the rain poured down. Had only three pupils, taught until dinner. Sewed on Maggie's dress this afternoon. Sitting in the twilight this evening pleasantly musing on this life of ours full of changes, memory bore me swiftly back to days long since flown, and then pointed to the future, its cares and aspirations, its doubts and misgivings. What may it not contain then for me? I sometimes think the past is a shrine containing the brightest part of my life, and then something bids me hope for what the future may bring. I feel as if I want to give vent to my pent up feelings when I look around and see all things so bright and beautiful — Yes all of God's works are beautiful, Earth, sea and sky. Why can we not appreciate it more than we do? We let so many trifles sour a life that might rejoice if we were not given to brooding, musing over the dispensation of a Divine Providence.

Wednesday July 1st 1868 — A warm bright day. Par has been sick all day, he was taken last night with a severe colic. Have done nothing much beyond teaching, sewed a little this evening. I feel warm and weary, will therefore be brief. Cousin William and Uncle Frank were here this afternoon.

Thursday July 2nd 1868 —— Taught as usual, feel weary in consequence of exerting myself so much in the schoolroom. Weary, yet I must not shrink from my duties or repine. I must work with the children here for the years are passing and they too will soon be men and women in this great arena of life. I have very little time to call my own but I will do my duty and there will be that calm the consciousness of right always brings. I went to Mrs. King's a short time this afternoon. Sewed on Maggie's sleeves.

Friday July 3rd 1868 — Very warm. The children sang this evening and seem much delighted. Dressed after school and sewed on Maggie's dress. Maggie and I took a short walk after supper. In my dreams last night some visions of past years, ere the first cloud had marred my life's young sky. Why is it, I often wonder? I should dream of one who loved me long ago, in dreams is always so reserved. Can it be in His bright home above he loves me less? The disparagement is great, he no longer of earth, I a sojourner here, meeting with all the grosser elements of nature. Oh God, what a phonomena is this life. Hope and joy each here have an end, the loveliest and best must pass unaware of the fragile roses of the past.

Note: Here appears to be a section of missing pages, and the next entry is a portion apparently written the last part of July 1868.

* * * * *

... Georgia, the other to Ginia. I wish I had written all I owe. I must try to write more tomorrow if I live and nothing happens to prevent. The days are passing swiftly by and if we have good luck, my Darling will soon be here. I want to see her so much to talk to her. I have read a greater part of the day when I was not busily employed. I want to read all I can. I take pleasure in nothing but religion, can be compared to a well stored mind.

August 3rd 1868 — Several days have elapsed since I wrote, a dull feeling prevented I suppose. Aunt Becca is now at home, came Saturday. I am glad she has come back. It has been raining every since yesterday afternoon. I sent a letter to Victoria today. Dismissed school at dinner, having only two pupils beside Maggie. Cousin John remained all night last night, left about ten o'clock this morning, came in the schoolroom and read with us before he left. Brought me his photograph yesterday. Ah me! a mystery there is at the bottom of the whole affair; What does that letter show but a loving woman's love, all thrown back as some idle toy, after being fully satiated with its possession. I don't comprehend, it bothers me, I must know more about it. Many questions I have to ask, many explanations to demand when time and opportunity offers. It is very evident he does not wish for her love now, and he it was that became alienated and wished a separation. Her words, her manner of expression attribute it all to him. Did he ever love, as he must have professed he did? If so, why did he become estranged without some weighty cause. I can see none, I am puzzled, I know not what to think or do. If I only knew everything, I could know better. Was it to pass off time? Surely he must have known his own heart, no trivial thoughtless boy, a man, deep-thoughted man, as he must know his own heart. No excuse for his age cannot pardon such a mistake if a mistake it was, and then to think the same demand should be made again, but from a different source. Ah! he should have thought well before acting the part over again. Wonder if he would do the same in this case. I am almost tempted to test it anyway. I can't reckon either would suffer much real heart sorrow from the operation. It speaks a tale of man's perfidy and woman's constancy, even after being treated with coldness, neglect by one whom she looked up to as the acme of all her aspirations, her heart's idol. Woman, how often deceived! Still you trust hoping on till the last spark of love and hope is crushed, eradicated by the very one who first taught thy young heart to trust, who spread a sunshine over your life, who gloried in encouraging dreams he might blight, without one sigh for the anguish it must cost without worry to know the struggle you brave alone, to make the world think you have not suffered or lost that confiding trust, that beautiful existence. I sometimes think all men are heartless, they care not even while searching for a love they pretend to crave. They like to flatter, poor weak confiding woman, she believes him true and joys that she is beloved. I fear my faith is growing dim. Oh, what is not one true noble man worth when found, but who can tell them, they are so few. I doubt if there are three existing in every community. I shall have to stop, I can't write without placing human nature in its worst light. I wish so much to find out all and will if I am spared. I know he will let me ask him and I believe he trusts me implicitly. Strange! though it is. Wonder, he does not wish to make the impression he never cared, I am sure his manner manifests such. I believe he thinks I doubt him, and he has a cause. I hardly know how to believe him (after all he has told me). I have never been deceived, thank God! even though I write thus, yet I have seen so much to make me distrust. Woe to that one who if ever a blight should be made after so many professions.

Tuesday August 4th 1868 — Raining this morning when I got up but soon ceased. It has been cloudy all day. This afternoon the rain poured in torrents. Broke up school today for vacation, don't know whether I will teach again or not. Sewed a little on Par's shirt, afterwards cut watermelon rind for preserve. Eddie came this evening and remains all night. Par went to Hampton today, came back to dinner. I feel dull and sleepy, do not feel like por-

traying the follies of mankind, am not in such a mood as I was
last night. I feel a calm sometimes creep over my whole system. At such times there is no incentive to urge me onward.
Levin has gone to Mr. Crandol's tonight.

Wednesday August 5th 1868 — It has been showery a greater part of
the day. Heard Maggie's lesson, notwithstanding I have given
vacation. Cousin William was here this morning. I sewed on
Par's shirt and got along considerably. Uncle Barnie and Mr.
J— Wilburn ate dinner here. Aunt Becca and Maggie went to
Mrs. King's this afternoon. Eddie left this morning after breakfast. Uncle Kit was here a short while this evening. I suppose
my darling will soon be here. I shall be so glad to see her, have
much to tell her. If it was in our power, how differently would
we make the lives of those we love. Every care should flee, no
dark waves of trouble should wash away the joys of life! But
then that would make this life too desirable. "Tis best as it is."
A Wise Providence has made all things for the best, though we
cannot comprehend it. I am getting very sleepy and must stop.
Have read considerable tonight in my papers.

Thursday August 6th 1868 — It has indeed been a lovely pleasant
day. I have been sewing very steadily all day, finished Par's
shirt. I feel so much better when I have been busily employed,
a calm content reigns in my heart. I feel I have been doing
something for those I love and that makes me happy. I try to
be useful, if I fail it is no fault of mine. Levin has gone to carry
Bessie to Mr. Croswell's. I suppose he thinks he loves, but I
fear he will find himself sadly mistaken. He is young, inexpe-
rienced, knowing nothing of the realities of life. I wish I could
see Sister, I feel oh! so much anxiety. I wish I could have a
good talk with her and Mrs. Stores, but I become overpowered
and cannot give vent to what I fain would utter. Ah, I fear
there is to be much unhappyness. I feel sad when I think of
it. Billie is so good and embitters his life, he can't be happy.
Oh my God, what would I not do for the sake of harmony and
giving peace to the Chosen one of my heart, he whose happiness I would value above all earthly gains, whose slightest wish
would be filled by me with an inward pleasure. All are not
alike, I would do all I could were it to sacrifice my own hap-

piness to obtain that peace, so essential to strengthen that love. That must be my stay through coming years. How I wish I could see her. I love her and feel sad if she is unhappy.

Friday August 7th 1868 — Commenced my dress body, nearly finished it. Cousin Mollie came this morning, staid only a short time. About dinner a party of Federal soldiers came down from Williamsburg under command of Captain Alston. I suppose they expect some depredation upon the citizens and have come to, if possible, avert it. It made me think so much of the past to see armed men. Olden memories were refreshed and the faces of some who are now sleeping in their grass grown graves were again before me. My heart felt a pang, a yearning for the days of yore. Happier was I in those days of suspense than now in this sad stern reality. I hoped on, prayed for the lives of those battling so nobly in our cause, and expected a final peace, blessed with their return. A peace did come, or what was called Peace in the national world, but oh! to many a sorrowing one there never came an opiate to soothe a heart crushed, its hopes its aspirations blasted, its light, its joy departed, never again to return. For when the war ceased, how many were left by kind comrades sleeping the last long sleep. Many were the vacant chairs, fond familiar faces appeared not among those who went out with stout hearts and full ranks. God knows the countless meek sufferers who still weep for the loved ones "that come not again" "Soldiers rest, thy warfare over. Sleep the sleep that knows no waking."

Saturday August 8th 1868 — A bright morning but clouded up and had quite a shower. Victoria came home this morning, a young man named Lee brought her. Aunt Becca and I went over to see her tonight. The rain came very fast and we had to come home in it. I felt a little damp about my shoulders. Sewed very steadily and finished my dress.

Sunday August 9th 1868 — Very beautiful. Did not go to church, attended to domestic duties all the morning. This afternoon Cousin John, Mr. Bennett, Mr. J. Hudgins and Mr. M. Hudgins were here. Mr. Bennett left about sunset. Cousin John and the

Messrs. Hudgins did not leave until after 9 P.M. Victoria came over after dinner.

Monday August 10th 1868 — Extremely pleasant. Mother has been much indisposed all day. I sewed on my chemise all the morning and a portion of the afternoon. Cousin William was here this morning. Lizzie came this afternoon, also Mrs. King and Victoria. Mrs. King took supper with us which was quite a treat. She is such a good kind old lady. Victoria and Mrs. King left about eight, Lizzie directly after supper. Promenaded considerably on the porch. I will hurry to bed as I expect it is growing late.

Wednesday August 12th 1868 — Did not write in my journal last night, had so much to do, could not find time. Mrs. Alston and the Captain and two other gentlemen stopped here all night. Ripped up one of my dresses this morning, sewed on Levin's shirt. Received a letter today from Darling and I am so very much disappointed she is not coming. I feel so very sorry but she thinks it best. It seems as if the fates have decreed that we shall not meet for a long time if ever. "Tis ever thus from childhood hour, I've seen my fondest hopes decay." Yes, it seems as if my most cherished plans meet with a blight. I had anticipated so much pleasure. Par went to Hampton today, sent Mother's bonnet.

Thursday August 13th 1868 — Very pleasant and bright. Sewed on Levin's shirt, made considerable progress. Cousin William was here this afternoon, staid some time in Aunt Becca's room. I felt exceedingly dull this afternoon, had no disposition to talk. I wish I could have gone off somewhere this summer, but I expected company, did not come, was therefore much disappointed. I fear Aunt Becca became offended at one of my remarks today but really, I meant not to offend. She, I don't think likes for me to say anything much, therefore I think I will try hereafter to not say anything that can at all offend although I had not the remotest idea of wounding her feelings, would not willingly do so. Hope I may be more guarded so as not to make any remark, however trivial, that can in any way tend to offend. Mother went to Mrs. Buchanan's this afternoon.

Monday August 17th 1868 — Several days have elapsed since I wrote. Friday night had company which remained so late it unfitted me for writing. How very strange it is he should profess to love me, I can't understand it, so very mysterious. He has promised to make an explanation of several items. Last night Cousin John, Mr. J— Hudgins and Mr. Malcolm were here. They all remained until eleven o'clock P.M. Went to church yesterday. Mr. Bennet carried me. We dined with Miss Lizzie Davis. Sewed on my lawn dress today. Sister and Brother Willie came yesterday. This afternoon Aunt Beccs, Mother, Sister and Maggie went to Mrs. Cook's. I staid at home. Cousin William came, joked me excessively.

Tuesday August 18th 1868 — A bright warm day. Wrote three letters this morning to send in tomorrow's mail. Mother, Sister and Maggie spent the day with Cousin Sarah. Sewed on my dress a little while. I am very sleepy, can't write at much length.

Wednesday August 19th — Quite warm. Mr. Hudgins and Cousin John spent the day here and set up our beds for us. Mr. Hudgins was very jocose relative to one of my friends. What an indifferent air he assumes now. The dream at last is over, such dreams must have an end. Love, hope and joy passes like meteors away. Again we press onward in search of new loves, and new joys ere the expiring embers have been removed or scattered by indifference from the shrine of our worship. I feel sad when I think of the love wasted, which might have been valued and guarded so carefully had it been bestowed, where it could have been reciprocal. I appreciate but cannot give in return, even were it tenfold unless possessing those attributes suited to my admiration. Sewed on my dress a little, hope I may finish it tomorrow. Mrs. King and Victoria came over after supper.

Thursday August 20th 1868 — I have felt very warm and dull all day. Sewed on my dress and finished it. Made a cake this afternoon. Sister, Maggie and I spent the evening with Victoria, had quite an agreeable time. It is quite rainy now. I must read and prepare for bed. I am sleepy and dull.

Friday August 21st 1868 — Did nothing much like sewing. Made custard to freeze for this afternoon as we expect some friends to spend the evening. They came, we had quite a nice time.

Saturday August 22nd 1868 — Very bright and pleasant. Have not felt well, laid down a short while. Expect to go to church tomorrow.

Sunday August 23rd — Mrs. Stores and Brother Willie came up early this morning and remained all day. Par and Brother Willie went to church this morning. Aunt Becca, Sister, Maggie, Georgie and I went this afternoon. Eddie Goffigan went with us, had quite a pleasant time. Mr. Bennett and Cousin John came up tonight. Mr. Bennett was as lively as possible. They left about 1/2 past 9 P.M.

Friday August 28th 1868 — Cloudy this morning but the clouds soon dispersed. Mother and Par left this morning for Hampton. Mr. Moss and Captain Alston remained all night here last night and took breakfast here this morning. Aunt Becca and I went to church tonight. Mr. Hudgins carried us. We had a very pleasant ride and enjoyed the meeting exceedingly. Came home about 11 o'clock P.M.

Saturday August 29th 1868 — Very warm and bright. Hemmed around the bottom of a coat for Georgie, hemmed a handkerchief for myself and attended to my domestic duties. Wrote a long letter to Lizzie this morning, hope to hear from her soon.

Sunday August 30th 1868 — A beautiful Sabbath morning. Par and Mother went to church this morning, came home to dinner. Aunt Becca and I then got ready and all of us went back with them in the afternoon. Had quite a nice time. The church was so crowded we should have found it difficult to get a seat but for the kindness of Mr. Hudgins. He gave us his and made some other gentlemen relinquish theirs. Cousin John has been here tonight. Mr. Hudgins came up tonight also and intends remaining all night to start for Norfolk in the morning. Cousin John left after 10 P.M. I feel sad when I think of some who have loved so deeply and still manifest an interest in me, notwithstanding my indifference. I want to see them happy even if I cannot be instrumental in bringing it about. I would not be

the cause of erasing every confiding feeling as I fear I might
have done, had I have let them known all at once, but I could
not bring my heart to the task. My sympathies were too deeply
aroused. I could not bear to wound, although I knew it must
be. A sigh heaves my breast when I think of his noble heart,
his truth, his forbearing love with what might seem a fickle-
ness on my part. God knows! how highly I respect him and
how! I feel for every pang I may have cost.

Monday August 31st 1868 — Very warm. Did not any sewing whatever. Commenced ripping up one of my dresses this morning.
Went to Dr. King's this afternoon. Sat on the porch sometime
after supper. It is a beautiful moonlight night. Everywhere as
far as the eye can reach looks indeed lovely. Sir John has not
returned yet. Received money this afternoon for Nicholas'
schooling.

Tuesday September 1st 1868 — Very warm all day, had a slight shower
this afternoon. After supper, Aunt Becca and I commenced to
get ready for church, but the clouds assumed such unpropi-
tious form, we thought it best not to start, and I am extremely
glad we did not for the rain afterwards poured in torrents
attended with much thunder and lightning. Sir John returned
tonight, brought me a very pretty bouquet. Commenced a pair
of pants for Georgie this afternoon. Victoria came after supper.

Wednesday Sept 2nd 1868 — The sky was clouded a greater part of
the day — this afternoon the sun shone out a little. I have been
sewing on Georgie's pants all day. Mr. Bennett came up this
afternoon and made an engagement to carry us to church to
the Lecture to be delivered there tomorrow by Mr. Martin. It is
still cloudy, the moon is shining faintly. I love to look at its
beams and ponder on nights that have passed when the moon
shone as brightly in the long ago, and my heart dreams were as
bright and free from care as the orb on which my eyes gazed.
Not that I am unhappy now for I try to be content, yet the
future can never bring hours more joyous, scenes more delightful, than those my heart learned to worship in the hours of my
early girlhood, ere I found the lovliest and best must fade away,
or thought how quickly I would learn a reality so stern, as to

make life seem for awhile a desert drear, and at best to teach the heart, although to learn the lesson of submission that its first love and hope were the best and lovliest, — far more! than after years have power to make.

Thursday Sept 3rd 1868 — The clouds passed off this morning and Mr. Bennett came to take me to the Lecture. I went; had a very nice time. Was much pleased with the discourse, which was on the "Character of the Nation." Returned home about 1 o'clock P.M. Sewed a little on Georgie's pants. We intended going to church tonight but the weather was too unfavorable. Mr. Bennett left after eight o'clock P.M. I must make haste and retire, as I feel a little dull.

Friday Sept 4th 1868 — The rainy weather has not cleared up yet, it poured in torrents this afternoon. Sewed on Georgie's pants. Aunt Becca and I have been holding a long confab since we came up to bed, about the conduct of a certain gentleman. Yes! I think I am justifiable in being cold toward him. I don't think he deserves hardly the most formal respect. I will let it be seen I tolerate no such acts, abhor them most intensely. He is not a man such as God designed should enjoy this false fair earth, but a desperate wreck of that true manhood; he might and could have made for himself, but for listening to the destruction promptings of an evil temptation.

Sept 5th 1868 — The clouds of yesterday disappeared and the Sun looked very bright this morning. Sewed a little during the day. I have felt dull and indifferent a greater part of the day, and even a little sad, as the thoughts of other days flitted o'er my memory as they sometimes do. When I allow myself to think, although it avails nought, I cannot recall one moment back again, or bring at my bidding one face, I loved to look upon save only in the silent shades of memory, filled with loved faces of the long ago.

Sunday Sept 6th 1868 — Very beautiful and pleasant. Spent the day quietly. This afternoon Mr. Hudgins came and remained until eight P.M. Mr. Hogg, Mr Bennett and Cousin John were here. The evening passed away very pleasantly in various chit-chat. They left after 9 P.M. Nothing of unusual interest has transpired. I will now read and make my usual preparations for bed.

Monday Sept 7th 1868 — Similar to yesterday. Sewed on those, never it seems to be finished pants. Mrs. Dunton spent the afternoon and staid until after supper. Willie ate supper here also. Annie Crandol and Ginia were here a short while this afternoon. Nothing of unusual interest has transpired. I had a very singular dream which I have thought much about. I want to see Mollie very much, will write to her tomorrow if nothing happens to prevent. I must also answer my Darling's letter, received last week. Who is the Herbert of my dreams to be? I can't imagine. Am I to have an ideal by that name? He must be something more than ordinarily attractive to win my love, that has never been bestowed but upon those in every way worthy of the best feelings of my heart.

Tuesday Sept 8th 1868 — Very pleasant all day. Finished those pants, commenced repairing one of Levin's shirts. Went to Mrs. Cooke's this afternoon. Spent a very agreeable time, although Lizzie was not at home. Yet I love to talk and hear old Mrs. Cook talk, she is so good, indeed both of them are. Wrote two letters tonight, one to Mollie and one to Darling. Hope to hear from both soon.

Wednesday Sept 9th 1868 — Exceedingly warm all day. Par went to Hampton, returned about five o'clock P.M. Went to Mrs. King's a short while this morning. Cousin Sallie Curtis was here this morning. Finished repairing Levin's shirts. Read right much in my paper received today. Victoria came over after supper. We sat some time in the porch, chatting as girls are apt to do. Mr. Crocker ate dinner here and later in the afternoon, Mr. Lively came from Yorktown. He and Mr. Dehart called for lunch. Today is the 7th anniversary of a day that I remember well, I have thought of often during the day. I wonder where they all are, those soldier friends who were with us then. Many – if not all of them have found a last long sleep on the battle plain, and those if any there be remaining are far away, grown reckless perhaps disparing over a "lost cause." How I should like to see them! even if it would refreshen olden memories, over which the lapse of years have failed to throw the dust of oblivion. Yet all these pangs of regret for the past would I forego, to see faces upon which I could gaze with a melancholy pleasure, enough to make the tear—drops start, and the sigh heave my bosom for the hopes that have been cherished and buried with the long ago.

Thursday Sept. 10th 1868 — The weather still continues hot. Today was Par's birthday. Made dessert for dinner. Did not have time to attend to any sewing until the afternoon, commenced a shirt for Par. I feel dull, will therefore be very brief tonight.

Friday Sept. 11th 1868 — Excessively warm. Aunt Becca, Maggie and I spent the day with Cousin Sarah. I sewed on Par's shirt, made considerable progress. I am so warm I will prepare for bed.

Saturday Sept 12th — Still the same warm weather. Sewed on Par's shirt again today and mended my stockings. Received a short letter from Sister this morning. Mrs. Stores has been sick, so she writes. Maggie has been complaining all day. Sister writes that Mollie has gone to Warwick and Mr. Nash accompanyed her. I wonder if he is loving her. How I should like to know all about it. I want to see her so very much! I wish she could meet with some true noble heart to lavish the wealth of her warm young heart upon, one who would prize it and make himself worthy of its passion, for she is worthy of a good husband. I want to see her happy, and am not so selfish as to be unwilling to resign her to one who made her life pleasant. This is a fleeting false fair life at best. Why then not seek to make those fast flying moments as happy as God designed it, instead of repining, wasting its mornings in vain regrets! I try to be content even if disappointments have shaded my pathway. It may be for the best. God alone knows what is good for his creatures.

Sunday Sept 13th — Very warm all day. Just as Mother was eating dinner, Uncle Barnie's wife and children came. They remain all night. Par and Maggie have both been quite sick all day. Maggie got up this afternoon but Par is quite sick now. We have had no gentlemen company as usual; it seems really strange.

Monday Sept 14 1868 — Sunshine and clouds this morning and this
afternoon the rain poured in torrents. Par has been quite sick
all day. Maggie had another chill today. Have done no sewing
whatever. Mrs. King (senior) is very sick. I feel very anxious
about her. Hope she may soon be better. Cousin Sidney is here
tonight.

Tuesday Sept 15th 1868 — The rain came slightly this morning, it
then ceased, but is still cloudy. Cousin Sarah sent for Aunt
Becca this morning, she and Uncle Kit both being sick. Par has
been quite sick today, but seems better tonight. Sickness is prevailing to a great extent all over the County. I went to see Mrs.
King this morning. She was asleep, consequently did not go up
to see her. Maggie missed her chill today. I hope it may be clear
by the morning for several reasons. I will write to Cousin
Martha soon.

Wednesday Sept 16th 1868 — Cleared off very beautifully this morning. Par is a little better. Thank God! Laura left after breakfast
this morning. I went to see Mrs. King this morning and she is
a little better. Read in my paper received today and sewed a
little on Par's shirt. I have a cold which makes me feel dull,
not at all in a writing mood. Wrote Sister a short note by Mr.
Lively.

Thursday Sept 17th 1868 — The temperature of the air has changed
very much since yesterday, and tonight it is very cool. Par has
been a little better today, but was right sick for a short while
this morning. We breakfasted very late, consequently the day
has passed away rapidly. Cousin William was here a short time
this morning, came in the cook room where I was churning,
seemed to have a disposition to chat, which I must have surely
evinced was decidedly distasteful. He thinks there is a change
in my manner (and well he might) for I deem it is time to
change, when he glories in what I consider is enough to tinge
his cheek, and gnaw his heart with remorse, the longest day
he lives. Received this afternoon a letter from Mr. Vaughan,
which surprised me exceedingly. I am undecided whether to
reply or not, he is so I don't know what. Mrs. Mary Cook spent

the afternoon with us. She and I went to see Mrs. King. She is better.

Friday Sept 18th 1868 — Cool mild and beautiful, a day for real dreaming of all that is lovely in earth, air and sky. How! my soul soars on wings of fancy, as I look around and everything speaks to my heart in a voice of alluring beauty, yet with a sadness mixed with all. So great is the spell, that Nature in all of her varied shades throws over my musings. Went to see Mrs. King as usual. She is better. Par is improving slowly. I sewed a little on a shirt today. Intended to write a letter or two tonight but Sir John came which prevented my doing so. We sat in the parlor in pleasant conversation. Sometimes he is still fond of joking me some. I feel for him, for I believe he still regards me with feelings of the deepest friendship, notwithstanding my indifference to a warmer feeling. I believe he has a generous warm heart, yet we cannot be more than friends. I wish to be friendly as long as life shall last. I would not sever the tie that binds us as friends, even if ties stronger (than might have been) have been riven by my own self, but not triumphantly or disquietly. No! No! I glory not in wounding a single heart even if I do distrust all mankind. Sometimes. Beneath all of that distrust there are feelings of finer nature, a sympathy, a sorrowing for those who are so unfortunate as to love where there is no responsive echo of my heart.

Saturday Sept 19th 1868 — The counterpart of yesterday. Have felt very dull all day. Did no sewing. Have been disappointed about going to see Mollie. This is the second time I have made an engagement without fulfilling. I don't care if it is a little cloudy in the morning, I fear she will think I did it purposely. Wrote a letter to Cousin Martha this morning.

Sunday Sept 20th 1868 — The sun shone brightly this morning, clouded up this afternoon. Mrs. Crandol and Kit were here a short time. Have had no company today. Mr. Bennett was here a short time this afternoon but I did not see him. It has been a dull day altogether. Mother has been much indisposed all day. Sister did not come as anticipated. Sir John, I heard was sick, consequently did not go to the Court House. I am sorry he is

sick, but am glad he did not come to go, as it was out of my
power to do so, and he might have attributed it to indifference
on my part, not willing to make an excuse for me when I fail to
come up to an engagement. Mrs. King (Jr.) was here a short
time this evening. I have felt very dull all day, and am heartily
glad the day is over. Perhaps it is not right for me to say so as
it is the Sabbath. I may not have spent it as I ought, or may
not have thoughts that should have had possession of my heart.
I feel sleepy, will read, and go to bed to dream.

Monday Sept 21st 1868 — Very cloudy this morning, fortunately did
not rain. Mother has been indisposed, consequently I have been
very busy. Mr. Wall came down from Williamsburg and brought
a lady convalescent from the Asylum. They stopped and called
for dinner, which soon I had prepared, left about two o'clock
P.M. Poor girl! how I do pity her! so entirely alone, without
Father or Mother, dependent upon a world as cold and false as
this! Mr. Wall took her to her guardian, who refused to take
her! What may not be thy destiny ere thy career is closed? Miss
Marvin came down with Mr. Wall. I went over to call on her,
Mr. Wall came back with me, remained all night. Received a
letter from Lizzie and one from Jennie.

Tuesday Sept 22nd 1868 — Little cloudy this morning. Mr. Wall took
breakfast here. I went over to Mrs. King's about 11 A.M. Mrs.
King (Senior) is better. Mended one of my dresses this evening.
Mrs. King (Junior) came over this afternoon. Heard today Mr.
Hudgins was very sick. I am so sorry, hope he may be better
soon. Sickness is prevailing to an alarming extent all over the
County. May a Kind Father watch over and lead them out of
danger. I have tried to write something for publication tonight,
but the mood will not come. I feel dull, depressed cannot frame
my ideas to suit my fancy. Will make preparations to retire that
I may be bright for the duties that await me on the morrow,
should I be spared to take my accustomed share.

Wednesday Sept 23rd 1868 — Cloudy and clear alternately. Sewed a
little after attending to domestic duties. Heard from Mr.
Hudgins this morning, he is a little better. I hope he may continue to improve until he finally restored to health. I always

feel so much anxiety for any particular friend when they are sick, for we know not but what their time is come to sever the "silver cord" and leave our hearts desolate. Have been writing a short sketch since I came in my room — will finish tomorrow night and mail it Wednesday. All the compensation I ask is its publication. If I succeed, I will write again. I feel tired, consequently cannot write much.

Thursday Sept 24th 1868 — Cloudy, very, this morning. Cousin Howard and Mr. Davis ate breakfast here. Cousin Howard then went for Miss Bowen who Par has hired to come and cook for us. Aunt Louisa will leave soon. I hope the young lady we have may suit us, as it will be so much better for us to have one that can attend to everything like cooking. Sewed right much on Par's shirt, will finish it tomorrow. Intended to write tonight but could not do so conveniently.

Friday Sept 25th 1868 — Clear and cloudy during the morning, cleared off toward noon. Finished Par's shirt. Have been writing again tonight. Cousin Howard ate dinner here. It is now pouring in torrents. Have not heard from Mr. Hudgins today, but hope he is doing well.

Saturday Sept 26th 1868 — Cloudy and cool. Wrote off my manuscript this morning, but did not mail it. Will do so Wednesday. Like Miss Lizzie very much, hope we may get along with her. I have not heard from Mr. H — today but hope he is improving. Received a letter from Cousin Georgia. I must write some letters soon as I have four to answer. Georgie went to the Cousins today. Will stop writing. I wrote so much this morning, I don't feel much in the mood.

Sunday Sept 27th 1868 — A cloudy quiet Sabbath. No one has been here except Alex and Uncle Barnie, they dined here. Heard today Mr. Hudgins was better, hope he may soon be well. Sister and Brother Willie are here, they came just before supper. Nothing of unusual interest has transpired to break the quiet calm. I forgot! Eddie has been here also, but remained only a short time. I shall be so glad when opportunity offers for me to go and see Mollie. I really want so much to see her.

Monday Sept 28th 1868 — Cleared off very prettily. Sister left after four o'clock P.M. I have done no sewing whatever. Went to see Mrs. King (Jr), is very sick. I feel very sorry for her. Have been reading tonight, feel dull, will retire.

Tuesday Sept 29th 1868 — Very bright and beautiful, real Autumn day. Almost made two collars. Cousin John spent a greater part of the day here. Went to see Mrs. King this evening, she is very sick. It is quite cool tonight and the moon is shining brilliantly. How I love such soft moonlight! casting shadows here and there — seeming to woo the heart from its cares, to bathe itself in the silent stream of deep sentimental thoughts. A yearning, a regret steals over my spirit, on such occasions, there is such a scene. "Some recollections of days that have as happy been" and the "star of hope" glimmers faintly as we think what may be instead of regretting "what might have been." The future may be unclouded, yet it can never bring the same old joy of long ago! The heart's first awakening, its earliest aspirations, are the brightest, choicest flowers that lie withered in the pathway, and not one in the future, though as beautiful, can ever be the same to me.

Wednesday Sept 30th 1868 — Indeed lovely! Finished my collars, and commenced ripping up a dress. Aunt Becca returned home today, and was much flustrated because her Bureau and other articles had to be moved, but we did the best we could. Yet how often all one can do is never appreciated, and the blame is bestowed upon those who are often the truest and the best. God knows! we try to do our duty, yet when there is an inclination to think otherwise, what does it avail? No sacrifice, however great, would only be considered mere nothing. Well! well! we have done our duty and that is sufficient. I was very much surprised to receive a letter from Mr. B—. He writes very strangely, I think. I don't know what prompted him to address a letter to me. He writes Mr H— is better. Oh how thankful I am that he is so much, or rather getting better. It should teach him a lesson to live nearer to his God! May He in His all wise mercy watch over, give him patience and strength to bear up under affliction. I know most persons are impatient. What does it avail? I feel sad tonight, I scarcely know how or why! A depression steals over me, and as I glance at the moonlight I feel sadder still. Oh God! this is part of life, to live, to love, and suffer. All things thou hast made beautiful, yet a yearning steals over me, an anxiety for the frailty of all that life holds dear. It is a glittering bauble, a waste through which we blindly grope our way, little knowing the ills that beset our weary feet, as we toil onward. God alone can watch over and lead our steps tonight. I thank thee, Oh Father, for the blessings Thou already has bestowed, and sometimes feel not a murmur should pass my lips, I, who have kind, loving hearts around me.

Thursday Oct 1st 1868 —— What can rival the beauty of a bright autumnal day — its golden sunsets, azure skies, and more than all its soft rich moonlight? Ripped up and smoothed out my dress, ready for cutting out, and commenced an apron for myself. Went to Mrs. King's a short time this afternoon, she is better. Par has been quite sick all day. I don't know why it is but Aunt Becca seems to misrepresent me in her very thoughts. I am sure if I spoke short, did she not look mad enough to have said much more? I tried to control myself, and did not know what I said could be so misconstrued. Yes, we did do as we thought for the best what yet all was unappreciated, the merest child could not have evinced more dissatisfaction at a thing so simple or let it suffice to teach me a lesson I will not soon forget. I will set a seal upon my lips if possible. I am such a fault finder. I will have nought to say, let things be as they may. I could not help from shedding tears this evening when I thought how badly I was misrepresented. God knows, I would not add one iota to her trouble, for I know she must feel sad and lonely. I would help her if in my power to do anything to bring her peace and comfort, but I know she does not think so. She looks upon me with an eye I sometimes think almost of dislike. I can't help, I know how careful I am, almost afraid to argue anything for fear of being considered cross, disagreeable. I have made up my mind from this night to pursue a different course, let come what will. If I speak to comfort, it is never appreciated, but always looked upon as a reprimand, which God knows it is not intended as such. I suppose it is so with the world, for I verily believe there are some people, if you were to spill your heart's blood for, they would still think it was not enough. I wonder how Sir John is now. Hope he is improving. I feel sad on such a night as this. When all things around look so beautiful, a charm steals over me making me feel a sad regret.

Bridge

between Tavey's thoughts and her activities

By taking away away much of the subjective writing in Tavey's diary, where she reveals her most private thoughts, we have a skeletal view of her various daily activities. This gives the reader a better picture of life, especially Tavey's life, in the last half of the nineteenth century, at the time of the Civil War.

Covering over five years, from 1863 to 1868, the diary portrays the younger Tavey as living rather comfortably with her family in rural Tidewater Virginia. Although she could hear gunfire from time to time, it seems that she was never exposed to the direct violence of war. We know that Yankee military men were in the area, as Fort Monroe in nearby Hampton was in Federal hands, and that they occasionally stayed as lodgers in her home.

Michael Cobb, Curator of the Hampton History Museum, says that this area of Virginia was quite secure at this time because of the Union's occupation of Fort Monroe. He says that she and her family would have lived a quite safe, but restricted, existence, as a blockade of the area was in place both during and after the war. It was difficult to have a constant supply of goods and food, and inflation was widespread with the loss in value of the Confederate dollar. Perhaps Tavey's family had an advantage because of her father's owning a general store across the road from their home.

Jean Clarke, Tavey's granddaughter, has information from her friend, Robert C. Emerson, a retired minister and historian, about Tavey's home: Pastor Emerson found in "Thomson's Mercantile and Professional Directory of Virginia," printed in 1851, a listing that George W. Smith was a "Hotel Keeper." Tavey's father had constructed another building to adjoin their residence by a covered portico. This was to serve as sleeping quarters for travelers. Jean Clarke likens it to a modern-day Bed-and-Breakfast or Guest House.

We see Tavey growing older in York County and putting her education to good use by becoming a teacher in her home. Although not everyone could read and write at that time (only about half the women), and public schools were not readily available, Tavey's family seems to have been literate. The education of children in rural areas took place in the home, in someone else's home or in one-room schoolhouses, where available. The subjects taught by Tavey to her younger students were likely reading, writing and basic arithmetic. The only book she mentions using in her classroom was the *Pinney Exercise Book*, although she does not say what exercises it offered. Her instruction may have been similar to the education she had received. *McGuffey Readers* were also available at that time, although quite new, as well as other texts. She also writes that she received money for her teaching.

Tavey also becomes a great help in the home and family business with her "domestic duties." She writes that she cleaned, made beds, planted, churned, cooked and baked, mended and sewed. Her parents undoubtedly relied upon her for her energy and ability.

She found great interest in the outside world beyond her home and neighborhood, and she savored her newspapers. She most likely read *Harper's Weekly*, the most popular paper in both the North and the South at the time. The tabloid-sized paper, printed in New York, was noted for its impartial reporting of the war and its graphics. Other newspapers she might have read were the *Washington Post*, The *New York Times*, *The New York Herald* and papers in Philadelphia and Baltimore that were also in print. Virginia papers that might have made their way into the area could have come from Richmond (the *Examiner*), Staunton or Lynchburg. It is possible that Smith's Store received newspapers to sell. Tavey also was likely exposed to newspapers from travelers stopping at the Smith home.

Tavey dealt from time to time with a sad melancholy, seemingly caused by an event that took place on September 9, 1861, when a young soldier, presumably Confederate, dies or is killed. She mentions it on September 8, 1868. Although the young man is unknown to us by name, Tavey gives us a small clue on February 27, 1868, by relating him to a Mrs. Williams. As Tavey felt quite alone in her sadness, she wrote about her despair, and she kept busy, which she said helped her. It is interesting to note that she wrote with compassion about meeting a young woman who was a patient at the "Asylum" in Williamsburg.

As communication was important to her, Tavey tries to keep in touch with others by visiting and by writing letters. She often mentions persons visiting her home, and she visits others. Mail was delivered by friends or family members or put into the country's newly-organized mail system at certain locations, perhaps at her father's general store.

Tavey's entertainment was limited. She mentions games she played, especially "charades," which resemble short skits. She also played cards, and she enjoyed having her fortune told. She ventured into the supernatural with cards or by looking into wells or on sand for images of some future boyfriend. Other than newspapers, Tavey mentions reading poetry and adventure stories. She paraphrases Byron in one couplet, and she mentions reading Tupper.

Tavey becomes interested in her religion. She mentions attending church often, on Sundays as well as during the week. According to historian Roane Hunt, three churches were near her home: Big Bethel Baptist Church was the place chosen by the local Confederate forces "as the most southern point of the defense on the Lower Peninsula against the Union forces out of Fort Monroe in Hampton." Another was the Grafton (a nearby community) Christian Church, which she calls the "Brick Church." Both of these churches were on the State Road / Old Stage Road that ran between Hampton and Yorktown. Tabernacle Methodist Church, located in the middle of Poquoson, a community a little south of her home, was the third church mentioned. She often attended services on Sunday, as well as during the week. This was not unusual, as churches were social centers for many families in both the South and the North, especially during the war. Two of these churches she attended were destroyed during the Civil War, and the third has long since vanished. She also mentions that she was very pleased to receive a Bible as a gift.

Tavey's transportation is also a consideration. For the most part, that would have been her two feet. Most people walked everywhere at that time. She also mentions wagons and carts and horses, as well as being "carried" to church. We can assume that this was in a buggy owned by a friend or neighbor, although we can assume that her father had a wagon and at least one horse. Water also provided a means of transportation, as ferries and steamers ran from Hampton, where Fort Monroe was located, to Norfolk and Baltimore at this time. She writes about her father taking trips to both cities.

Finally, Tavey is interested in marriage as it was likely expected of her, especially as she became older. We know that over 400,000 troops supporting the Confederacy were killed in the Civil War, which certainly limited the supply of available young men. Even so, Tavey had a number of suitors, most of whom she found unsuitable. Her heart still seemed heavy with longing for her long-ago soldier.

Thus, we see Tavey in the activities that filled her days. She spends a good part of the last year of the diary, 1868, sewing. Perhaps this was a creative outlet for her artistic abilities, as she seems to sew and mend and crochet without complaint.

Finally, Tavey usually describes the weather at the beginning of each entry. It is very similar to the weather of southeastern Virginia today.

A brief skimming of the following abbreviated entries and observations from her diary offers a better understanding of Tavey's living in her head and in her heart. It seems to have helped her to survive the challenging circumstances of her life and time.

TAVEY'S DIARY (ABRIDGED):
WHAT SHE DOES

1863

Tavey reflects upon the events of the past year of 1862 on the Virginia Peninsula. Apparently, Union forces had invaded the area. General Stuart (J. E. B.) and his raiders had been on the north side of the Rappahannock River, some 70 miles from Tavey's house. Tavey seems to be a Southern sympathizer.

Th, Jan. 1 — "We carried a letter" (to Louisa Turner)

F, Jan. 2 — "...Still the heart seems void in every pleasure...." Neighbors visiting was a form of both communication and entertainment.

Sa, Jan. 3 — Tavey's weather observations are constant entries in the diary. Her strong religious convictions are also seen here and will continue.

Su, Jan. 4 — Letters received came largely from neighbors and friends.

M, Jan. 5 — Tea was a part of the daily ritual of many as a carryover tradition of English colonists, who settled in this area in the early

17th century. Tea was usually served between two and five o'clock.

"....the laughing face is not always an index to the heart...." Tavey's depression becomes apparent here and will be seen throughout her diary. Tavey seems to have lost a friend.

Tu, Jan. 6 — "....a sad foreboding (is) still around me...but there are reasons for it which are useless to dwell upon." Tavey, it seems, has been told to get over her melancholy.

W, Jan. 7 — Tavey's concern for the soldiers might indicate that she had had contact with one or more of them.

Th, Jan. 8 — Tavey recalls the March 9, 1862, naval battle between the Union's "Monitor", a wooden ship covered with iron, and the Confederate "Virginia", formerly the Union's "Merrimack." The "Merrimack" had been scuttled by the Union, resurrected by the Confederates and covered with iron at Gosport Navy Yard in Portsmouth, across the harbor of Hampton Roads from the Peninsula. The battle was inconclusive. Union forces had also taken Vicksburg, Mississippi, and Murfreesboro, Tennessee.

F, Jan. 9 — Tavey reads about the battle at Murfreesboro and mentions Gen. Rains.

Sa, Jan. 10 — Tavey gives "praise and thanks" for the success at Vicksburg.

Su, Jan. 11 — Tavey mentions ..."Mrs. Cooke's servant (Caroline)." Southerners called their help "servants," whether they were slaves, indentured or paid.

M, Jan. 12 — Tavey's sadness is evident again.

W, Jan. 14 — Remembering a year ago, Tavey becomes despondent at hearing of General Magruder's success.

Th, Jan. 15 — Tavey reads more war news about Galveston in a newspaper.

Sa, Jan. 17 — Tavey hears or reads about the battle at Holly Springs, Mississippi.

M, Jan. 19 — Tavey reads the "Southern Almanac," a publication printed in 1863 and 1864 in Lynchburg, Virginia.

Tu, Jan. 20 — Tavey mentions two Yankee officers and a "Union friend" of someone in her house.

Th, Jan. 22 — Tavey's father brings a newspaper from Hampton.

Sa, Jan. 24 — The family in some way receives another newspaper.

Su, Jan. 25 — Tavey writes a letter to a friend today.

M, Jan. 26 — Tavey rolls a friend's hair.

W, Jan. 28 — Tavey receives a newspaper from a "Yankee Captain" and delights in General Burnside's problems. A friend tells their fortunes.

Fr, Jan. 28 — Tavey and friends practice their "charade."

Sa, Jan. 31 — Tavey and friends perform their charade. The family reads about a Southern naval success in "a Yankee paper."

**

Su, Feb. 1 — A newspaper tells them of another Southern naval victory.

Mo, Feb. 2 — Tavey hears about Vicksburg and a Confederate victory at Blackwater, Virginia.

Mo, Feb. 9 — Tavey hears or reads of General Magruder's activities in Texas.

Tu, Feb. 10 — The family finds a newspaper. Yankees are in the neighborhood.

Sa, Feb. 14 — Tavey hears that Norfolk has burned.

W, Feb. 18 — Tavey receives a wedding invitation.

Th, Feb. 19 — A neighbor returns home after detainment at Point Comfort (Fort Monroe), about fifteen miles away, for a week. The family receives a newspaper and reads about Napoleon.

F, Feb 20 — The family receives a newspaper, but "no news of importance."

Su, Feb. 22 — Tavey notes the "anniversary of our illustrious Washington's birthday." Tavey relates the latest adventure of the "Alabama."

Tu, Feb. 24 — Tavey reads poetry.

Th, Feb. 26 — A friend "will carry my letter."

Sa, Feb. 28 — Relatives walk to see Tavey and her family.

**

Mo, Mar 2 — Tavey plays "charades" again. Tavey hears about a capture and Vicksburg.

Tu, Mar 3 — Tavey reads of battles near Strasburg in Western Virginia. (West Virginia became a separate state in 1863.

W, Mar 4 — Tavey notes the "second anniversary since the Abolition President (i.e., Lincoln) assumed office," and praises "Our President, Jefferson Davis" for a proclamation setting aside "a day of fasting...." for "given us the victory."

F, Mar 6 — The family could not find a newspaper.

Sa, Mar 7 — The family found a newspaper and read of the burning of a Confederate steamer.

M, Mar 9 — Tavey is sewing.

Tu, Mar 10 — Tavey's uncle brought a newspaper, where the family reads of some Confederate victories in Tennessee.

Th, Mar 12 — Uncle Kit brought another newspaper to the family.

F, Mar 13 — Tavey returns a crochet needle.

Tu, Mar 17 — Tavey received a paper with reports of victories by the Yankees, which she does not believe, and some captures by the Confederates.

W, Mar 18 — Tavey is 18 years old today, although she does not seem to celebrate it.

Su, Mar 22 — Tavey hears of the death of a family friend.

F, Mar 27 — Tavey notes the day is that "appointed by President Davis for fasting and prayer." The family receives a Yankee newspaper, which tells of a skirmish involving slaves in Georgia.

Sa, Mar 28 — The family receives a Southern newspaper citing Confederate victories in Tennessee.

**

M, Apr 6 — Tavey receives "a present of a Bible." The family receives a newspaper, and Tavey is "thankful" for a Yankee defeat.

F, Apr 10 — Tavey visits friends. She reads about both a Yankee and a Confederate disaster in a newspaper.

Sa, Apr 11 — Tavey hears "cannonading towards Williamsburg."

Tu, Apr 14 — "Cannonading has been heavy…." Tavey writes.

Th, Apr 16 — Tavey's uncle brings the family a newspaper with war news.

F, Apr17 — Tavey hears that "Our (Confederate) forces are in possession of Williamsburg."

Sa, Apr 18 — Tavey reads that the "Yankee fleet has left Charleston."

Su, Apr 19 — Tavey hopes that "our forces have surrounded Suffolk." She also hears "heavy cannonading" and is "all anxiety to hear from it."

Th, Apr 23 — Tavey's uncle brings her a note, and she returns articles requested by him.

Sa, Apr 25 — Tavey plants "flower seed...."

Su, Apr 26 — Tavey's family receives a newspaper with more war news.

Th, Apr 30 — Tavey's friends and cousins plan "to go after snails tomorrow...."

**

F, May 1 — Girls "went after snails" and "put our snails in plates of meal."

Sa, May 2 — The coming of Spring causes Tavey to recall a year earlier and to become sad.

Su, May 3 — Tavey reads more war news in a newspaper. Mollie "intends teaching school."

M, May 4 — Tavey remembers the evacuation of Yorktown one year ago. She is sad.

F, May 8 — Tavey hears that Yankee papers report "a severe battle at Fredericksburg...."

Sa, May 9 — Tavey hears that "We have again repulsed the Yankee Gen. Hooker."

Tu, May 12 — Tavey hears that "Gen. Jackson is wounded in the left arm...."

F, May 15 — Tavey hears of a battle near Fredericksburg with heavy losses on both sides. She also hears that "Gen. Jackson is dead." She is sad.

Sa, May 16 — "Par went fishing today."

Su, May 17 — "Levin carried Sister and myself...."

M, May 18 — "Par is much indisposed today...."

Th, May 21 — "(W)e looked down the well...(and) saw a man's image...."

F, May 22 — She reads in papers that "...Public speakers in the city of New York are denouncing Lincoln's administration...."

Sa, May 24 — "Mr. Segar made a speech today at the tabernacle... and they are going to rule entirely by Yankee rule."

Tu, May 26 — "Several Yankees came today in search of one of their horses."

Th, May 28 — "An election was opened at the Halfway House, for members of Congress."

Sa, May 30 — "Par went fishing...."

Su, May 31 — "...(O)ur places of worship have been demolished....not more than two places where services can be held."

**

Tu, June 2 — A paper says that "the Yankees have again been repulsed at Vicksburg."

W, June 3 — "... three Yankees... searched the kitchen for arms."

Th, June 4 — A paper gives "late news from Vicksburg.... We have also sunk the gunboat *Cincinatti*.... How grateful we should be...."

Th, June 11 — Tavey reads in a paper that "The Yankees seem confident...."

W, June 17 — "Three Yankees came...and searched the house."

F, June 19 — Tavey reads in a paper that "Gen. Lee is invading Md. and Penna."

**

F, July 10 — "Several weeks have lapsed.... quite a number of changes...." "(T)he Yankee's say we are defeated...."

**

F, Aug 21 — "More than a month has intervened...."
"Today has been set apart by out President as a day of fasting and prayer."

**

M, Sep 20 — "O how sad and lonely I sometimes feel.... I review the past with deep regrets."

**

F, Oct 24 — "I must think well and think deeply...."

1864

Jan 14 — Tavey remembers "Just this night two years ago...oh, how many changes since that happy period."

**

Feb 3 — "I don't know why or what has come over my feelings of late....Is it the old sad forebodings visiting again my once happy heart?" Tavey's gloom returns.

Feb 15 — An unknown drama has occurred here.

Su, Feb 21 — "...Have I not my thoughts...my constant companions...."

"...the present...is obscured by the clouds of what may be called sorrow."

**

Sa, Mar 5 — "I feel weary, sad and almost lonely."

Mar 19 — "Yesterday was my birthday. It hardly seems probably that nineteen years have elapsed...."

"I wonder if I shall feel much happier my next birthday if I am living...."

"I hope our Southern homes will be prospering under the blessings of peace...."

"I am sometimes addressed (as).... 'Old Lady.'"

Mar 25 — "My heart feels sad...."

**

Apr 1 — Tavey's sadness continues.

1865

Apr 4 — "A year has elapsed..., and today I sit saddened and almost despairing."

Tavey is teaching and lists her students and books here.

(First lessons in *French for Children* by Mrs. Barbault, *Pinney Exercises with Key.*)

"A woman's love will endure forever....Destroy it and her happiness has departed, never again to return!!"

(Editor's note: President Lincoln is shot on April 14 and dies on April 15 in Washington, D.C.)

1866

Mar 18 — "My birthday, I have been spared to see twenty-one years...."

"...I stand upon the eve of a maturer life...."

"May I not find some heart to which my own can respond.... No No! there is none like him."

**

July 5 — "The Picnic of the fourth is over. I enjoyed it very much...."

"That hour's conversation changed the light frivolous feelings of the girl into a determined woman...."

"I cannot love him and therefore must not ever think of marrying him."

July 13 — "I feel wounded and depressed in spirit. The heart is weak...."

1867

Feb 18 — Has Tavey been jilted? Is Tavey trying too hard to find love?

**

April 1 — "Today two weeks ago (March 18) was my 22nd birthday."

"I could not love where it was not mutual.... I pray it may never be my fate." Tavey is remembering her first love, but has she lost a second love?

**

June 9 — Tavey mood deteriorates again.

**

Aug 13 — "The leaves in my life's history are being slowly but surely
unfolded. What will happen next?" Tavey has been shocked by
something.

**

Nov 2 — "Memory, sweet noiseless memory, how oft do you bear me
back to happier days than now, when all was bright and beautiful in this life of ours...."
   "... know I must have loved, or I could not now repine." Tavey
thinks that she is getting older, and she prays that "I learn to do
thy will and meekly bow whenever thou seem fit to chasten."

1868

Tavey has been writing again, but many pages are missing. This
begins in the middle of an entry begun in early 1868.

Tu, Jan 14? — "... all... ate egg and salt hoping to see the partner of
our joys and sorrows." Tavey still has hope.

W, Jan 15 — "...I am beloved."

Th, Jan 16 — "What a season for dreaming girlhood is....I turn to
the past where commenced my first dreams of love...."

Su, Jan 19 — "Cousin John came this morning...." Is he a real
cousin?

M, Jan 20 — "The letter puzzles me beyond expression."

Tu, Jan 21 — Tavey is "making a dress for Mother." She is also writing letters.

Th, Jan 23 — "I feel so much happier when I have been usefully employed." She also plays the piano.

F, Jan 24 — "Finished Mother's dress today, also a pair of drawers tonight, it took me only six hours to make them."

Su, Jan 26 — Tavey received two newspapers and a letter from Darling, a loving friend. "Sir John came this evening...."

M, Jan 27 — "A rainy day, cut out a dress body for Mother...."

Tu, Jan 28 — "Finished a pair of drawers tonight and... wrote a letter to Darling."

W, Jan 29 — "....(W)e grow old forgetful of the time.... Have finished Mother's body, sewed on Maggie's dress and afterward made tatting and read."

F, Jan 31 — Her friend Mollie is concerned about her mother.

**

Sa, Feb 1 — "Sent a letter to Darling...and received a letter from Cousin Levin...."

Su, Feb 2 — "Mrs. Fletcher left for Hampton...."

M, Feb 3 — "Have been very busy all day braiding a yoke...."

Tu, Feb 4 — "Finished braiding my yoke today.... Wrote two letters tonight.... I have been thinking of writing a composition.... I sometimes feel quite poetical.... The past contain all of my most precious heart gems.... The present seems too like a stern reality.... I... know and feel the happiest days of my life have passed.... I write as if I am growing old."

W, Feb 5 — "... my journal began... today 6 years ago. I can scarcely realize it so swiftly, yet so sadly have those years flown...."

Th, Feb 6 — "Finished braiding my sleeves, and commenced embroidering.... Kindly beams are they (that)...shine...on all the pure and holy...and are the lonely vigil that keep watch over many a lone and distant grave of beloved ones far, far away."

Sa, Feb 8 — "Wrote two letters this morning.... Received no paper today...."

Su. Feb 9 — "...read Tennyson, and my Bible.... I see the faces of those who loved me in days of yore.... I feel the first bud of love, its first young leaves are faded, withered. The brightest star there has set. The clouds arose and brought a storm to crush many a girlish as well as matron's heart...."

M, Feb 10 — "Par left for Baltimore this morning. Cousin Howard went with him to Hampton. He brought me two papers and a letter.... Have been embroidering on my yoke today, and tonight have been reading in my papers...."

W, Feb 12 — "...Have been embroidering during the day, read Tennyson and tonight made tatting."

Th. Feb 13 — "... Embroidering again today.... Sir John came this afternoon ...and did not leave until 11 o'clock P.M... Par returned safe and well...."

F, Feb 14 — "... Many are the sentimental and comic flatteries have been going on today! I expect some tomorrow as it is mail day...."

Sa, Feb 15 — "Received a paper today.... Made a little necktie for Mr. B. for a Philopena.... Have received no valentines as yet."

Su, Feb 16 — "...Several gentlemen were here this evening...."

M, Feb 17 — "Have been embroidering all day, and reading.... I try to pursue the path of rectitude and duty. I heard today of a poor girl who has fallen from all that makes life desirable...."
Tavey is concerned for the young woman.

Tu, Feb 18 — "Embroidering today as usual...."

F, Feb 21 — "...Have finished my yoke and have been sewing on my chemise today."

Sa, Feb 22 — "...made a pudding for dinner, made yeast and sewed a little on Mother's dress...the birthday of one of Virginia's noblest Sons, heard no firing of cannon. Nothing to remind one of the great Hero."

Su, Feb 23 — "Attended to my domestic duties as usual this morning...." Company came later.

M, Feb 24 — "Finished Mother's dress and sewed sleeves in my chemise... My yeast worked beautifully today...."

Tu, Feb 25 — "My light cake was a failure.... Sewed on my chemise this evening...."

W, Feb 26 — "...Commenced braiding a yoke today...."

Th, Feb 27 — "The gloom of yesterday still prevails... I have fondly today viewed ...scenes of bygone joys...."

F, Feb 28 — "...Have been braiding today on my yoke...." Tavey dwells on ill friends.

Sa, Feb 29 — "Received a paper and two letters... Made pastry and cakes this morning...."

**

M, Mar 2 — "...Commenced a sun bonnet for myself...."

Tu, Mar 3 — "Cooked breakfast again this morning. Aunt Louisa... came in after breakfast and attended...to her work... I never feel lonely when I am busy. Almost finished my bonnet...."

W, Mar 4 — "Finished my sunbonnet...and commenced braiding. Brother Willie came with the mail...."

Th, Mar 5 — "Braided on my yoke this morning and read all the afternoon.... Mrs. Curtis was to be carried to the Asylum today... How horrible it must be for Mollie to see her only Parent so affected...."

F, Mar 6 — "Finished braiding my yoke and nearly finished stitching it. Had the kitchen room upstairs scoured out as I expect to teach school Monday... Sir John brought me a letter from Mrs. Stores...."

Sa, Mar 7 — "Wrote four letters this morning... Mended a little this evening... Received my paper this morning...."

Su, Mar 8 — "...Have enjoyed myself so much today!... Tomorrow I commence my school duties...."

M, Mar 9 — Tavey is in a fine and philosophical mood.

Tu, Mar 10 — "Mother and Par left early this morning for Hampton... Have been braiding on my sleeves...."

W, Mar 11 — "The day has passed as usual, finished one of my sleeves and commenced another... Have been cutting bed quilt pieces since supper. Today was the birthday of one of my dear friends, had he lived to see it... I know his rest is blissful for he was good and true...."

Th, Mar 12 — "...Have been braiding my sleeve and doubtless would have finished had I not stopped to wind some cotton. After supper cut bed quilt pieces...."

F, Mar 13 — "Finished braiding my sleeve, and made two neck bows... I composed, wrote some verses on Levin's birthday, which is tomorrow. Afterwards pieced on my quilt...."

Sa, Mar 14 — "Received a letter and a paper... I have been darning all day...." Tavey seems sad again.

Su, Mar 15 — "Wrote to Mollie this morning and sent the letter by Mr. Hudgins...."

M, Mar 16 — "Arose very early this morning to attend to some domestic arrangements, cut out a chemise after breakfast and almost made the body. Eddie came...and told my fortune for me with cards... Read Tupper ...this afternoon...."

Tu, Mar 17 — "Arose early ...and cooked breakfast. Aunt Louisa was sick. Cooked dinner also, sewed a little on my chemise. Read Tupper...this afternoon. I try to employ my time usefully...."

W, Mar 18 — "My birthday. 23 years... Many may think me happy as I ...wear the mask of calm content. Yet none know how deep in my heart is a grave.... Will the flowers of love and hope bloom again(?)... Time alone will tell... I wonder if I live how I will feel next birthday, if I will be gliding down the same monotonous stream...almost finished my chemise...."

Th, Mar19 — "Finished my chemise and commenced some crochet trimming... Have not commenced teaching yet...."

F, Mar 20 — "I wrote a short composition this morning, will try to correct it tomorrow, and...will make an attempt to have it published. Crocheted a greater part of the day...."

Sa, Mar 21 — "...Did not receive my paper as usual this morning...much disappointed... Have been mending my drawers...."

Su, Mar 22 — "...Sir John brought my letter...."

M, Mar 23 — "Commenced a bosom for Par and crocheted a little....Received my paper....Victoria...brought me a book to read called the 'Wandering Guerrilla'...."

Th, Mar 26 — "Left my ink downstairs consequently did not write last night as usual. Made another bosom for Par....Cousin Georgia...has been relating some interesting anecdotes relative to the days of our young Confederacy. I sigh for those times...."

F, Mar 27 — "...Nearly completed one of Par's shirts... Maggie sleeps with me now...."

Sa, Mar 28 —— "...friends forget the cares of the world come between
the loves of earth, and who professes to be a friend today, tomorrow may be a foe.... I played one tune... Made pies and custards
this afternoon for dinner tomorrow."

M, Mar 30 —— "...Have finished one of Par's shirts.... Par went to
Hampton today, and brought my paper."

Tu, Mar 31 —— "...I sat upstairs all the morning waiting to see the
bridal party pass... Have been sewing on Par's shirts and reading tonight."

**

W, Apr 1 —— "Thoughts of beautiful bright days with flowers of
beauty rise in the imagination at the word (April)...."

Th, Apr 2 —— "Have been sewing as usual...."

F, Apr 3 —— "Par went to Hampton this morning, did not bring any
letter for me.... Finished Par's shirt."

Sa, Apr 4 —— "Mended a greater part of the day...."

Mon, Apr 6 —— "Par and Mr. Hudgins left early this morning for
Norfolk. Have been busy all day making a shirt for Levin, sewed
as long as I could see...."

M, Apr 13 —— "A week has elapsed since I last wrote. Have been to
Hampton.... Crocheted a little trimming for a little shirt...."

**

Su, May 3 —— "Aunt Becca and I anticipated going to church but was
disappointed...."

M, May 4 —— "Cloudy, cool day, a day of gloom without and
within...." Tavey prays for the sick Maggie.

W, May 6 — "Did not write in my journal last night, had the headache so very badly.... Sewed and finished a night gown shirt...."

Th, May 7 — "... Did not have but two pupils today, consequently dismissed school at dinner.... Read right much this afternoon...."

F, May 8 — "....school. Commenced braiding on Aunt Becca's sleeves. Maggie seems better... George is very unwell tonight. I bathed his feet, rubbed his breast in mustard...."

Sa, May 9 — "... Have done no sewing al all. Wrote a sketch off entitled 'In the Twilight'. I intend finishing it and attempt to have it published... Read a part of the day in my papers...."

Su, May 10 — "...a beautiful day for church... Sir John...drew my photograph on the wall."

M, May 11 — "Cloudy and rainy. Did not have but two pupils today... Sewed on my nightgown this afternoon, braided on Aunt Becca's sleeve in school... I told their fortunes (Victoria and Mr. King)... Par was very much worried as he wants his horse to plow."

Tu, May 12 — "... All of my pupils except my little Darling and Georgie were present. Have done no sewing whatever...."

W, May 13 — "The rain poured in torrents. I had only one pupil to come. Sent him home.... Received a letter in the mail this morning from Emily.... We have never met since we parted seven years ago, long and dreary years. Many are the changes since then.... The War had actually commenced, but none of its direful effects were felt...."

Th, May 14 — "A day of bright sunshine... I thought it enough to make the soul forget its realities of sorrows and toils...."

F, May 15 — "... Braided on Aunt Becca's sleeve during school hours...."

Sa, May16 — "Mended my dress.... Wrote two letters...."

M, May 18 — "... Made two cakes this evening, one a sponge, the other a butter cake...."

Tu, May 19 — "... Finished one of Aunt Becca's sleeves, commenced my night gown sleeves."

W, May 29 — "...Have done nothing...except my school duties.... Received my paper today...."

Th, May 21 — "Braided on Aunt Becca's other sleeve in school...."

F, May 22 — "...Made my nightgown sleeves after school... I feel dull, dull...."

Sa, May 23 — "...Hope we may go to church tomorrow...."

Su, May 24 — "...Mr. Bennet came and carried Aunt Becca and I to the brick Church. I enjoyed it very much... We arrived home about ½ past 2 P.M... Ah who can tell! What a day may bring forth... I believe he loves me...." This entry must be read, as it indicates a great change for Tavey.

M, May 25 — "... Made some crochet braid trimming for Mother... I feel like I am right again"

Tu, May 26 — "...finished my crochet trimming... I sigh, I know not why!" Tavey writes of deception here.

W, May 27 — "... I have paid two visits this afternoon... so little I go out. Taught school as usual...."

Th, May 28 — "...Commenced repairing my light dresses...."

F, May 29 — "...Fixed one of my summer dresses after school"

Sa, May 30 — "...Aunt Becca and I expect to go to church tomorrow...."

Su, May 31 — "A beautiful Sabbath, went to church as anticipated
...."

**

M, June 1 — "Summer is here or at least the summer month... I am
so glad we can go to church tonight...."

Tu, June 2 — "... Aunt Becca and I went to church as anticipated...Cousin John's curiosity was unbounded yesterday
relative to my journal. I brought it down to show him a piece
in there about the Picnic... I am very sorry he read it...."

W, June 3 — "... Taught as usual, sewed on Maggie's baby dress...."

Th, June 4 — "... Sewed on Maggie's baby dress... The workmen are
still here building...."

F, June 5 — "... Sewed again on Maggie's dress. After school Aunt
Becca and I made 41 cakes for the Store... I must really write
my MS. And send it for publication...."

Su, June 7 — "... Aunt Becca and I went in the cookroom and fixed
dinner for (Mr. Bennet)...."

M, June 8 — "Several of my pupils were absent today. Crocheted
during school hours, commenced repairing one of my
dresses...my time is so entirely engrossed with my school and
domestic duties."

Tu, June 9 — "... Finished repairing my dress, and commenced fixing another."

W, June 10 — "The 7th anniversary of our famous 'Bethel battle.'"

Th, June 11 — "... Repaired one of my dresses and commenced a
lawn dress for myself. Aunt Becca is making the skirt for me...
I did not teach school, the weather was too inclement for any
of the children to come."

F, June 12 — "... Made ruffles for my sleeves... Had only three pupils, consequently dismissed earlier."

Sa. June 13 — "... After going trough the routine of my domestic duties, sewed on my lawn dress. Aunt Becca finished the skirt for me today... Alex Tabb ate dinner here... After dinner, Aunt and I made a cake for tomorrow's dinner...."

Su, June 14 — "A beautiful Sabbath. Made boiled custard for dinner... I was so much heated over the stove, Mother did not think it prudent for me to go (to church)...."

M, June 15 — "... Crocheted a little today... My little Darling commenced school today."

Tu. June 16 — "...taught as usual... Received two letters this evening...."

W. June 17 — "... Sewed on my dress body after school...did not sleep well last night....."

Th, June 18 — "...Crocheted during school, sewed on my dress body, and...read History. I have suddenly lost all interest in light literature. My mind craves something deeper."

F, June 19 — "... Sewed very little today.... Major Putnam and another Yankee stopped for supper and lodgings. I had to hurry and make beds for them."

Sa, June 20 — "After going through my usual routine of dusting and cleaning, sat down to my sewing and finished my dress... Alex ate dinner and supper here...."

Su, June 28 — "more than a week has elapsed...during which time I have been in Hampton; went to the Picnic... Went to Hospital Point on the Portsmouth side... Came back to Hampton about 7 P.M. Arrived at home to dinner today...."

M, June 29 — "Arose early...and commenced my usual school and domestic duties... I felt sad and depressed tonight...."

Tu, June 30 — "...Had only three pupils, taught until dinner. Sewed on Maggie's dress this afternoon...I sometimes think the past is a shrine...."

**

W, July 1 — "Par has been sick all day...with a severe colic. Have done nothing much beyond teaching, sewed a little this evening...."

Th, July 2 — "Taught as usual, feel weary in consequence of exerting myself so much in the schoolroom. Weary, yet I must not shrink from my duties... I have very little time to call my own but I will do my duty...."

(Some pages are missing here.)

End of July — "I must try to write more tomorrow if I live... I have read a greater part of the day, I want to read all I can... I take pleasure in nothing but religion...."

**

M, Aug 3 — "Several days have elapsed since I wrote... Dismissed school at dinner, having only two pupils beside Maggie... I sometimes think all men are heartless... They like to flatter, poor weak confiding woman, she believes him true and says that she is beloved. I fear my faith is growing dim... I have never been deceived, thank God...." This passage must be read for whatever Tavey is saying or not saying.

Tu, Aug 4 — "...Broke up school today for vacation, don't know whether I will teach again or not. Sewed a little on Par's Shirt, ...cut watermelon rind for preserve...."

W, Aug 5 — "... I sewed on Par's shirt... A Wise Providence has made all things for the best, though we cannot comprehend it... Have read...tonight in my papers...."

Th, Aug 6 — "...I have been sewing very steadily all day, finished Par's shirt. I feel so much better when I have been busily employed, a calm content reigns in my heart...."

F, Aug 7 — "Commenced my dress body, nearly finished it... About dinner a party of Federal soldiers came down from Williamsburg... Olden memories were refreshed... My heart felt a pang, a yearning... Happier was I in those days of suspense than now in this sad stern reality... A peace did come...." This passage must be read for Tavey's view of the end of the War.

Sa, Aug 8 — "...Sewed very steadily and finished my dress."

Su, Aug 9 — "...Did not go to church, attended to domestic duties all the morning...."

M, Aug 10 — "...I sewed on my chemise all the morning...."

W, Aug 12 — "...Ripped up one of my dresses this morning, sewed on Levin's shirt. Received a letter today from Darling and I am so very much disappointed she is not coming...." (Who is Darling?)

Th, Aug 13 — "Sewed on Levin's shirt...I fear Aunt Becca became offended at one of my remarks...."

M, Aug 17 — "Several days have elapsed since I wrote... How very strange it is he should profess to love me, I can't understand it... Went to church yesterday. Mr. Bennet carried me... Sewed on my lawn dress today...."

Tu, Aug 18 — "...Wrote three letters ...to send in tomorrow's mail... Sewed on my dress...."

W, Aug 19 — "...The dream at last is over... we press onward in search of new loves... Sewed on my dress a little...." We wonder at the drama that has taken place with Tavey.

Th, Aug 20 — "... Sewed on my dress and finished it. Made a cake this afternoon...."

F, Aug 21 — "... Made custard to freeze for this afternoon as we expect some friends...."

Sa, Aug 22 — "...Have not felt well... Expect to go to church tomorrow."

Su, Aug 23 — "...Par and Brother Willie went to church this morning. Aunt Becca, Sister, Maggie, Georgie and I went this afternoon....

F, Aug 28 — "...Aunt Becca and I went to church tonight. Mr. Hudgins carried us...Came home about 11 o'clock P.M."

Sa, Aug 29 — "...Hemmed around the bottom of a coat for Georgie, hemmed a handkerchief for myself and attended to my domestic duties...."

Su, Aug 30 — "...Par and Mother went to church this morning...all of us went back with them in the afternoon...I feel sad when I think of some who have loved so deeply and still manifest an interest in me, notwithstanding my indifference...."

    We surmise that Cousin John has approached Tavey and has been rebuffed.

M, Aug 31 — "...Commenced ripping up one of my dresses this morning...Sat on the porch...after supper...Received money this afternoon for Nicholas' schooling."

    **

Tu, Sept 1 — "...Sir John,,,brought me a very pretty bouquet. Commenced a pair of pants for Georgie...."

W, Sept 2 — "...I have been sewing on Georgie's pants all day... Mr. Bennett came...and made an engagement to carry us to church to the Lecture...tomorrow by Mr. Martin...I try to be content...."

Th, Sept 3 — " ...Mr. Bennet came to take me to the Lecture ...which was on the "Character of the Nation." Returned home

about 1 o'clock. Sewed a little on Georgie's pants. We intended
going to church tonight but the weather was too unfavorable..."

F, Sept 4 — "...Sewed on Georgie's pants. Aunt Becca and I have
been holding a long confab... about the conduct of a certain gentleman... I think I am justifiable in being cold toward him...."

Sa, Sept 5 — "...Sewed a little during the day."

M, Sept 7 — "... Sewed on those, never it seems to be finished
pants.... I had a ...dream which I have thought much about...
Who is the Herbert of my dreams to be? I can't imagine... He
must be something more than ordinarily attractive to win my
love...."

Tu, Sept 8 — "... Finished those pants, commenced repairing one of
Levin's shirts...."

W, Sept 9 — "... Par went to Hampton.... Finished repairing Levin's
shirts. Red right much in my paper received today... Today is
the 7th anniversary of a day that I remember well, I have
thought of often during the day...." Tavey remembers the war
and becomes sad.

Th, Sept 10 — "...Today was Par's birthday. Made dessert for dinner...(and) commenced a shirt for Par...."

F, Sept 11 — "...I sewed on Par's shirt, made considerable
progress...."

Sa, Sept 12 — "...Sewed on Par's shirt...and mended my stockings...Mollie has gone to Warwick and Mr. Nash accompanyed
her. I wonder if he is loving her....I wish she could meet some
true noble heart...I try to be content even if disappointments
have shaded my pathway...."

Su, Sept 13 — "...We have had no gentlemen company as usual; it
seems really strange."

M, Sept 14 — "... Par has been quite sick...."

Tu, Sept 15 — "... Sickness is prevailing... all over the County...."

W, Sept 16 — "... Par is a little better. Thank God!... Read in my paper received today and sewed little on Par's shirt...."

Th, Sept 17 — "...Cousin William was here... (and) came in the cook room where I was churning...."

F, Sept 18 — "Cool, mild and beautiful, a day for real dreaming of all that is lovely in earth, air and sky... I sewed a little on a shirt today...we cannot be more than friends...."

Sa, Sept 19 — "... Did no sewing...."

Su, Sept 20 — "... I...am heartily glad this day is over. Perhaps it is not right for me to say so as it is the Sabbath...."

M, Sept 21 — "... Mother has been indisposed, consequently I have been very busy. Mr. Wall came down from Williamsburg and brought a lady convalescent from the Asylum (in Williamsburg)... Poor girl! How I do pity her!...." Tavey meets and takes pity upon a young woman, presumably mentally ill.

Tu, Sept 22 — "...Mended one of my dresses this evening...Sickness is prevailing...all over the county... I feel dull, depressed...."

W, Sept 23 — "Sewed a little after attending to domestic duties... Have been writing a short sketch – will finish tomorrow night and mail it Wednesday. All the compensation I ask is its publication...."

Th, Sept 24 — "...Cousin Howard...went for Miss Bowen who Par has hired to come and cook for us. Aunt Louisa will leave soon...Sewed right much on Par's shirt, will finish it tomorrow."

F, Sept 25 — "...Finished Par's shirt. Have been writing again tonight...."

Sa, Sept 26 — "...Wrote off my manuscript this morning, but did not mail it. Will do so Wednesday...."

Tu. Sept 29 — "... Almost made two collars...the moon is shining... How I love such soft moonlight!...A yearning, a regret steals over my spirit...."

W. Sept 30 — "Indeed lovely! Finished my collars, and commenced ripping up a dress...I feel sad tonight...A depression steals over me...Oh God! This is part of life, to live, to love, and suffer...." Tavey suffers frustration and offers a prayer.

**

Th, Oct 1 — "What can rival the beauty of a bright autumnal day....? Ripped up and smoothed out my dress, ready for cutting out, and commenced an apron for myself... I will set a seal upon my lips if possible. I am such a fault finder...I have made up my mind from this night to pursue a different course...I feel sad on such a night as this...a charm steals over me making me feel a sad regret."

TAVEY - AFTER THE DIARY

We leave Tavey, or maybe Tavey leaves us. No other diaries or writings by her have been found. We know that Tavey's brother, George, died December 22, 1868, two months after her last entry. He was seventeen years old.

Tavey does not reveal what "different course" she decides to follow. We can assume that she continued her "domestic duties" and normal activities. We know that she had met Alex Tabb, as she mentions his having dinner at her home on January 31, 1868, and visiting the family with her Uncle Barney later in the year. He is also mentioned in June as having meals with the family.

Perhaps Alex was either a good substitute for her lost love or a good friend. From research done by historian L. Roane Hunt, we know that he was born in 1845, presumably in York County, Virginia, to Mary Eaton and William Tabb. By 1854 it appears that he was an orphan. In a will recorded in York County, Hunt notes that William Tabb named Mathew Barney Smith as guardian of his son, Alex. This was Tavey's Uncle Barney, brother of her father. In the 1870 census, Hunt further tells us, Alex Tabb was listed in the household of Barney Smith in Warwick County, Virginia, which was on the James River a few miles west of Smithville.

We know that Alex Tabb of York County, Virginia, served in the Confederate army during the Civil War, as the family has a copy of his Oath of Allegiance to the United States, "as prescribed by the President in his proclamation of December 8th, 1863...in conformity with instructions from the War Department...." The Oath of Allegiance was required of imprisoned Confederate soldiers before release to "support, protect and defend the Constitution and Government of the United States against all enemies, whether domestic or foreign...(and) bear true faith, allegiance and loyalty to the same, any ordination, resolution or laws of any State, Convention or Legislature to the contrary notwithstanding;..." From this document we are also told that Alex had a dark complexion, dark brown hair and hazel eyes. His height is listed as five feet and seven-and-a-half inches tall.

The family also has Alex's Certificate of Release of Prisoner of War from Head Quarters, Point Lookout, MD, dated June 21, 1865. We do not know if he had been wounded in battle or where or when he was captured. We also do not know Alex's occupation upon his release from the military prison, although we know that he was in York County. He likely farmed, either fulltime or part-time, as almost everyone did. His circumstances would likely have been most interesting, if not romantic, to Tavey.

We know that Tavey married Alexander C. Tabb on April 4, 1871, two-and-a-half years after the last entry in her diary. We know nothing of their courtship or friendship. She was 26 years old

We also know that George W. Smith, Tavey's father, died on December 17, 1872, and left Tavey his property south of the road, while her brother and sister retained the property north of the road. As Tavey's inheritance was the land that held her home and ordinary or "guest house," she likely continued that business. She and Alex became the parents of three children, Howard, William and Margaret. (Howard Tabb was the father of Jean Clarke and Mary Elizabeth Hambleton.) Alex died in 1877, when he was 32 years old. It was not uncommon for Civil War veterans to suffer an early death because of the harsh conditions and disease suffered during their war years.

Tavey, a young widow and single mother with three young children, William, Howard and Margaret, must have kept very busy. We know that she received more property in York and Warwick counties from Rebecca W. King, the "Aunt Becca" she mentions so often in her diary. According to Roane Hunt, Rebecca W. Chisman is recorded as living in the Smith household in the 1870 census. "Becca," at that time the widow of George W. Chisman of Warwick County, later married Miles Henry King of York County. She no doubt inherited the property from both of her husbands and/or her father.

On December 31, 1893, about sixteen years after her husband's death, Tavey was commissioned Post Mistress of Tabb, Virginia, the area formerly known as Smithville. The post office was located in her home.

Tavey died in 1924, at the age of 79. She never remarried.

Billie Paxton Einselen

The Community and Family
of Mary Octavia Smith Tabb

By Roane and Phyllis Hunt

Mary Octavia Smith, or "Tavey" as her granddaughters refer to her, wrote this diary mostly in 1863 during the Civil War and in 1868, several years after the war. Mary Octavia was born on March 18, 1845, and lived with her parents, George W. Smith and Mary Anne Howard, in York County, Virginia, in the area of "Smithville," less than one mile northwest of the Halfway House on the Old Stage Road from Yorktown to Hampton.

Mary's father's land was purchased from John R. Crandol by his father, Levin Smith. Levin came to York County from Accomack County, Virginia, on the Eastern Shore. He married three times and bore children by two of his wives. His descendants are shown in the diagram on pages 124 and 125.

Mary's father, George, was born in York County to Levin's first wife, Margaret Savage. Besides Mary Octavia, George and Mary had five other children, and they are referred to on a number of occasions in Mary's dairy.

Levin Smith's three sons of his second marriage to Mary Rachel Hubbard, as indicated in the diagram on pages 124 and 125, were also born in York County, and their families are also mentioned in the diary. Benjamin Franklin Smith was "Uncle Frank," and Mathew Barney Smith was "Uncle Barney."

The 1850 York census lists George W. Smith, head of household, to be a merchant. Frank and Barney are listed in the household as clerks. This indicates that Mary Octavia lived in close relationship with her uncles.

The diagram, shown on page 127, of Mary Octavia's ancestors includes familiar names in York County's history, i.e. Savage, Howard, Calthrope, Russell, Hunt, and Langston as well as Smith. Also, the diagram shows Mary Octavia's grandfather, Levin Smith, who married her grandmother, Mary Hunt. In 1835, Levin Smith, born 1791, married Mary Hunt, born 1795. It was Levin's third marriage and

FAMILY OF LEVIN SMITH

Levin Smith, b. 1791, d. 1848
+m. 1st **Margaret Savage**, b. abt 1797, d. 1823

    George W. Smith, b. 1820, d. 1872
    +m. **Mary Anne Howard**, b. 1820, d. 1908

        Washington Lafayette Smith, b. 1842, d. 1843

        Sarah Frances Smith, b. 1843, d. 1912
        +m. William J. Stores, b. 1841, d. 1914

        Mary Octavia Smith, b. 1845, d. 1924
        +m. Alexander C. Tabb, b. 1845, d. 1877

        Levin S. Smith, b. 1847, d. 1905
        +m. Sarah Teresea Phillips, b. 1848, d. 1924

        George Smith, b. 1851, d. 1868

        Margaret Lee Smith, b. 1861, d. 1936
        +m. Fayette Smith Collier, b. 1854, d. 1931

+m. 2nd **Mary Rachel Hubbard**, b. 1804, d. 1834

    Benjamin Franklin Smith, b. 1828, d. 1895
    +m. **Sarah Elizabeth Phillips**, b. 1834, d. 1877

        Levin James Smith, b. 1852, d. 1909
        +m. Fannie Cary Curtis, b. 1855, d. 1892

        Robert F. Smith, b. 1854, d. 1915
        +m. Alice Diana Drummond, b. 1854, d. 1935

        Edward Barney Smith, b. 1856, d. 1933
        +m. Elizabeth Ann Croswell, b. 1857, d. 1939

        Ida Smith, b. 1858, d. 1883
        +m. James Vaughn Jones, b. abt. 1853

Mary's fifth. It followed that in 1841, Levin's son, George W. Smith, married Mary's daughter from a previous marriage, Mary Ann Howard.

Mary Octavia mentions many uncles, aunts, and cousins in her diary, some of which were in her Smith family. To determine if the other relatives mentioned were connected to her mother's family, the author searched the works of Mrs. Thelma Hansford on the Howard

Sallie Phillips Smith, b. 1862, d. ?
+m. Edwin Allen Sinclair, b. 1855, d. 1925

Aylmer Pelham Smith, b. 1864, d. 1925
+m. Josephine Bunkley, b. 1864

Charles Carrol Smith, b. 1866, d. 1938
+m. Josephine Mabel Groom, b. 1864, d. 1922

Mary Hubbard Smith, b. 1870, d. 1936
+m. Joseph Nathaniel Clark, b. 1868, d. 1939

Harry Gordon Smith, b. 1877, d. 1965
+m. Maggie Palmer, b. 1878, d. 1965

Matthew Barney Smith, b. 1830, d. 1887
+m. 1st **Lucy Curtis**, b. 1831, d. 1853
+m. 2nd **Laura Lee**, b. 1840, d. 1914

Anna E. Smith, b. 1865, d. 1902
+m. Wyatt B. Walker, b. 1860

Sada Smith, b. 1867, d. 1927
+m. George T. Garrett, b. 1861

Lucy L. Smith, b. 1870, d. 1886

Franklin B. Smith, b. abt 1872, d. 1927
+m. Elizabeth B. Jones, b. abt 1878

Florence E. Smith, b. 1874, d. 1922
+m. Zachariah T. Jones

Barney H. Smith, b. 1879
+m. Lillian Nock, b. 1885

James Augustine Smith, b. 1832, d. 1869

+m. 3rd **Mary Hunt**, b. 1795

family of York County. (A technical point to remember is that alternate spellings of Howard are Harward and Harwood.) The author was unable to identify any Howard relatives of Mary Octavia living in close proximity to Smithville. Her mother was the only child of Edward C. Howard, Jr., and Mary Hunt. The family of Edward Calthrope Howard, Sr., shows the possible Howard relatives of Mary Octavia. The siblings of Edward, Jr., were Thomas, Frances, Martha, and Lucy. Generally, the descendants of Thomas and Frances, who married Charles Lockey Collier, lived in Elizabeth City County, Virginia. Martha married John Harwood (another spelling of Howard) and lived in Warwick County, Virginia. Lucy did not marry. Of course, portions of Elizabeth City (Hampton) and Warwick Counties, adjacent to York County, were not far from Smithville.

Members of the King family were often mentioned in the diary. They were very close to the family. Dr John King was listed in the 1850 census records as living in the George W. Smith household. Dr. King's family was listed at the same time as living with his mother in Elizabeth City County. It may be that Dr. King was beginning a new medical practice in "Smithville," and it was not practical to have his family living with him in York County. The 1860 census lists Dr. King with his own household that included his mother. The diary mentions the entire King family if we assume that John Revere King was the "Sir John."

Another frequent reference in the diary was to an aunt as "Aunt Rebecca" or "Aunt Becca." This probably was the Rebecca W. Chisman that lived in the Smith household in the 1870 census record. She was the widow of George W. Chisman of Warwick County. Later, she married Miles Henry King, brother of Dr. King. Deed records show that Rebecca W. King gave property in York and Warwick to Mary Octavia Tabb in 1879 and 1883, respectively. There is no further indication that Rebecca was a blood relative of Mary Octavia Tabb.

The Cooke family lived adjacent to the George W. Smith home, and were frequently referenced in the diary. The William G. Cooke family was listed in the 1860 census along with his mother Elizabeth. All are included in the diary from 1863 to 1868. The Cooke and King family diagrams show the marriage of Elizabeth Sarah Cooke to Granville King. Also, Stafford G. Cooke, brother of William G. Cooke, settled in the Yorktown area of York County. The diagram includes one of his daughters, Anne, because she married William Edward Goffigan, who was mentioned in the diary. These are some of the names mentioned in the diary and some are located on the map shown later on pages 134 and 135.

Mary Octavia began her diary on January 1, 1863, eighteen months after the battle at Big Bethel. She expresses much sadness and hurt in her thoughts of war and its effects upon her life. September 9, 1861, was a special date when Confederate soldiers died.

ANCESTORS OF MARY OCTAVIA SMITH TABB

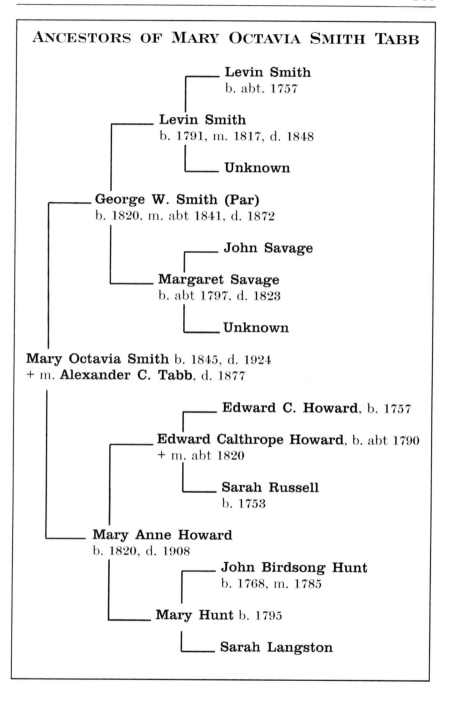

Levin Smith
b. abt. 1757

Levin Smith
b. 1791, m. 1817, d. 1848

Unknown

George W. Smith (Par)
b. 1820, m. abt 1841, d. 1872

John Savage

Margaret Savage
b. abt 1797, d. 1823

Unknown

Mary Octavia Smith b. 1845, d. 1924
+ m. Alexander C. Tabb, d. 1877

Edward C. Howard, b. 1757

Edward Calthrope Howard, b. abt 1790
+ m. abt 1820

Sarah Russell
b. 1753

Mary Anne Howard
b. 1820, d. 1908

John Birdsong Hunt
b. 1768, m. 1785

Mary Hunt b. 1795

Sarah Langston

She wrote of this in 1868, evidently because that special soldier died that she had favored and for whom she continued to grieve. Also, she related him to a Mrs. Williams as she wrote about him on February 27, 1868. Further search may one day reveal the identity of this special soldier who touched the life of this young girl and inspired such deep feelings.

Mary Octavia Smith married Alexander C. Tabb on April 4, 1871, four years after the last recording in her diary. Alex was the son of William Tabb and Mary Eaton, but by 1854 he was an orphan. In a will recorded in York County, William Tabb made Mathew Barney Smith guardian of his son, Alex. In the 1870 census, Alex Tabb was listed in the household of Barney Smith in Warwick County, Virginia. Mary probably met Alex through her Uncle Barney. She mentions Alex in her diary beginning on January 31, 1868, as taking dinner. He continued his visitations throughout 1868, sometimes coming with her Uncle Barney. As indicated in the diary, Mary had other suitors, but her heart was too heavy to commit to any of them.

After the recordings in the diary ended in October 1868, two very important events occurred in her life. First, on December 22, 1868, her brother, George, died and after she married in 1871, her father died on December 17, 1872.

Alexander Tabb served in the Civil War. He was imprisoned at Point Lookout, Maryland. His certificate of release and his signed oath to the United States are presented on pages 137 and 138.

Mary Octavia and Alex Tabb had three children: William, Howard, and Margaret. Their children and grandchildren are listed on the diagram on page 132. Like many other Civil War veterans, Alex died young after six years of marriage.

Mary Octavia Smith Tabb retained the Smith property south of the main road, and her brother and sister received the Smith property north of the road. Many years after the passing of Alex, Mary Octavia became the first Postmistress of Tabb Post Office on December 31, 1893. Her certificate presented on pages 140 and 141 is for a Postmaster modified with a "she" in place of "he" and "her" in place of his." Mrs. Jean Clarke is very proud to have the original certificate framed on the wall of her home.

Prior to the Civil War, cartographers of the U.S. Coast Survey Department were assigned to the Union Army to prepare war maps. A remarkable map was drawn of York and Elizabeth City Counties that shows great detail of Smithville. The portion of the map on pages 135 and 136 shows the Poquoson River from Howard's

---

FAMILY OF EDWARD CALTHROPE HOWARD

Edward Calthrope Howard, Sr., b. 1757, d. 1810
+m. **Sarah Russell,** b. 1753, d. 1815

    Thomas Calthrope Howard, Sr., b. 1780, d. 1824
    +m. **Ann __?__**

        Thomas Calthrope Howard, Jr.
        +m. Tabby Cropper

        Joseph C. Howard, b. 1804
        +m. Mary Ann Buchanan

        Edward Howard

        Robert Howard, b. 1811
        +m. Margaret Ellen Tennis, b. 1818

    Frances Calthrope Howard, b. 1783
    +m. **Charles Lockey Collier, Sr.**

        Henry Collier

        Charles Lockey Collier, Sr., b. 1824, d. 1863
        +m. Martha Wright Jones, b. 1828, d. 1818

    Edward Calthrope Howard, Jr., b. abt 1786
    +m. **Mary Hunt,** b. 1795, d. 1848

        Mary Ann Howard, b. 1820, d. 1908
        +m. George W. Smith, b. 1820, d. 1872

    Martha T. Howard, b. abt 1790
    +m. **John Harwood,** b. 1787, d. 1837

        William Edward Harwood, b. 1819
        +m. Rebecca __?__, b. 1830

        Benjamin W. Harwood, b. 1826
        +m. Martha E. Dunn

    Lucy W. Howard, b. bef 1794

[Harwood's] Mill on the left to its mouth on the right. Specific location are indicated by numbers identified in the table on page 135. The old stage road is shown from Big Bethel Baptist Church [1] passing by the Halfway House near the center [3] to the Grafton Christian Church at the top [13]. Mary Octavia wrote her diary dur-

---

FAMILY OF DR. WILLIAM KING

William King, d. 1828
+m. 3rd **Esther Shivers**, b. 1793, d. 1879

   Dr. John Curle King, b. 1821, d. 1889
   +m. **Mary E. A. Jones**, b. 1825, d. 1906

      Victoria Louisa King, b. 1845
      +m. Edward M. Lee, b. 1843

      John Revere King, b. 1848

      Granville S. P. King, b. 1855, d. 1924
      +m. Elizabeth Sarah Cooke, b. 1856, d. 1926

   Miles Henry King, b. 1824
   +m. 2nd **Frances L. Fox**, b. 1828
   +m. 3rd **Rebecca W. __?__**, b. 1820

---

ing the time that she lived with her parents at location [8]. The residences of the King [6] and Cooke [7] families are indicated nearby.

Mary Octavia made many references in her diary to church attendance. Her residence was central to three distinct churches in her community. The first, Big Bethel Baptist Church [1], was the location chosen by the Confederates as the most southern point of the defense on the Lower Peninsula against the Union forces out of Fort Monroe in Hampton. The first major land battle of the Civil War occurred at Big Bethel on June 10, 1861. The second was the Grafton Christian Church [13], which she refers to in her diary as the "Brick Church." The third church was the Tabernacle Methodist Church [16] indicated on the right side of the map, which was located in the center of the Poquoson peninsula. These were the churches available to Mary Octavia and to which she refers.

It is very important to remember that this map was prepared for the Union Army, and therefore, the various houses displayed were thought to be significant from a military perspective. The names given to each house were not the official record, but the name associated with each house as determined by Union sources. The greatest detail on the map was along the old stage road. Significant locations included the Halfway-House, Rosedown Estate, Russell Mill, George Smith's Store, Howard's Mill, Poor House Farm, and Grafton

Christian Church. Also, the mapmakers included the dwellings of medical doctors.

The "Smithville" portion of this map is shown in greater detail on page 136. This portion seems to have been drawn to illustrate Mary Octavia's diary. Again, the residence of George W. Smith [8], Dr. John King [6], and William G. Cooke [7] are indicated. Dr. King's residence is located above the Smith house, next to the road. The George Smith Store is indicated directly across the road from Dr. King. Next to the store is Miss Crandol, probably the dower of widow Crandol when Levin Smith purchased the land from the John R. Crandol estate. Location [4] is the original colonial site of the Charles Parish Glebe. After the Revolutionary War it was obtained by the Presson [Preston] family, later, by Thomas Smith who married Rebecca Presson, and eventually, by the Taylor family who are the present owners.

Across from the glebe and south of the stage road is the dwelling that the map—maker labeled as, "Reb. (Brassy) Preston" [5]. "Reb" was probably short for Rebecca, but could be Robert. This house was probably part of the Presson Estate. "Rosedown" [2] and the Halfway House [3] are indicated on left side of the map. Mary

FAMILY OF WILLIAM COOKE

William Cooke, b. 1786, d. 1847
+m. **Elizabeth Gibbs**, b. 1793, d. 1871

    William G. Cooke, b. 1818, d. 1884
    +m. **Mary F. Gibbs**, b. 1833, d. 1906

        John G. Cooke, b. 1850, d. 1911

        Elizabeth Sarah Cooke, b. 1856, d. 1926
        +m. Granville S. P. King, b. 1855, d. 1924

        William H. Cooke, b. 1858
        +m. Hattie P. __?__, b. 1878

    Stafford G. Cooke, b. 1820, d. 1894
    +m. **Sarah Gibbs**, b. 1824, d. 1882

        Anne Cooke, b. 1846, d. 1905
        +m. Wm. Edward Goffigan, b. 1841, d. 1909

FAMILY OF MARY OCTAVIA SMITH TABB

Mary Octavia Smith, b. 1845, d. 1924
+m. **Alexander C. Tabb**, b. 1845, d. 1877

    William Tabb, b. 1872, d. 1951
    +m. **Rosa Alma Thomas**, b. 1884, d. 1956

        Roslyn Howard Tabb, b. 1907, d. 1986
        +m. Charles Dixon Hudgins, b. 1898, d. 1989

        Lucille Alma Tabb, b. 1908
        +m. Jessie Lee Moore

        Virginia Elizabeth Tabb, b. 1910, d. 2005
        +m. Henry Edward Thomas

        William Stores Tabb, b. 1914, d. 1976
        +m. Rosalie Cooper, b. ?, d. 1999

        Annie Lee Tabb, b. 1918, d. 1968
        +m. Karl Gazurek

        Edward Thomas Tabb, b. 1920
        +m. Helen Gazurek

    Howard Tabb, b. 1875, d. 1930
    +m. **Maria Elizabeth Hoxie**, b. 1901, d. 1990

        Mary Elizabeth Tabb, b. 1925
        +m. Edgar A. Hambleton, b. 1918, d. 2005

        Jean Cary Tabb, b. 1928
        +m. William Samuel Forrest, b. 1924, d. 1993
        +m. B. T. Clarke, b. 1925

    Margaret Tabb, b. 1877
    +m. **Fred Randall**

Octavia made reference in her diary to the events held in the Halfway House.

North of the Poquoson River are the residences of John Wainwright, Curtis Messick, and the Lindsay family. The Poor House [12] is shown beyond the Wainwrights. Also, Yorkville is shown as the residence of John T. Wheeler from Elizabeth City County (upper right side of the map). Closer to the Smith's Store is the residence of William Bartlett [9], a lumberman from Massachusetts who was a leader in Big Bethel Church. Also, he was mentioned in the diary.

Next to him is John R. Thomas who had married the daughter of Christopher Curtis, referred to in the diary as "Uncle Kit." The Curtis Estate [10] is indicated to the left of this map, but can be seen in the larger portion, shown on page 136. Thomas Miles Curtis, son of Christopher, was also mentioned frequently in the diary.

The diary includes the names of many persons that crossed the mind of Mary Octavia. Some names were distinct and clearly referred to known relatives and neighbors. Others names are not distinguished clearly enough for definite identification. Also, it is interesting that many of the names are included in these rare maps.

Mary Octavia Smith's diary is a masterpiece. She reveals the heart of a young woman who has seen heartache at a very young age and in troubling times. She has recorded vignettes of history to be handed down for generations. She is poetic in her use of words and expresses herself in ways beyond her years. This diary is truly a treasure.

We appreciate the willingness of Mary Octavia's granddaughters to share this very personal diary of 1863–1868.

Home of Howard Tabb, son of Mary Octavia, in Smithville. Renovated building is numbered "6" in maps.

Union Army Maps of Civil War – Big Bethel to Grafton

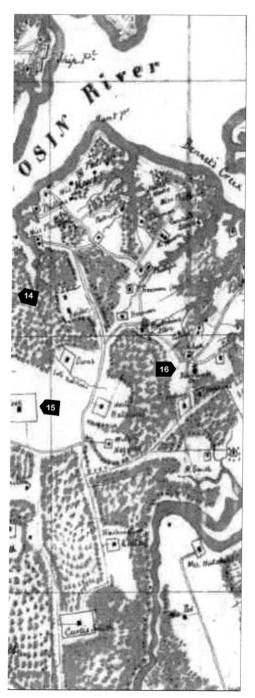

LEGEND

1. Big Bethel Baptist Church

2. Rosedown Estate – Home of Col. Thomas Russell

2a. Russell Tide Mill

3. Halfway House

4. Charles Parish Glebe – Owned by the families Presson, Smith and Taylor

5. "Reb. (Brassy) Preston" – Presson family

6. Residence of Dr. John King

7. Residence of Wm. G. Cooke

8. Residence of George W. Smith, father of Mary Octavia Smith Tabb

9. Residence of William Bartlett

10. Residence of Christopher Curtis

11. Howard [Harwood's] Mill

12. Poor House Farm

13. Grafton Christian Church

14. Residence of William Croswell, Calthrope Neck

15. "Thropeland"

16. Tabernacle Methodist Church

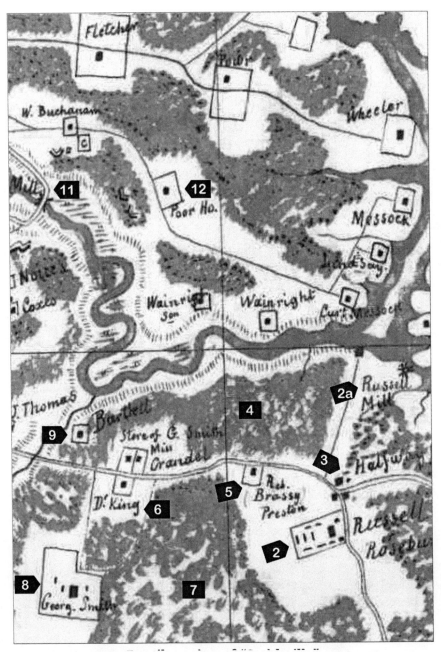

Detail portion of "Smithville"

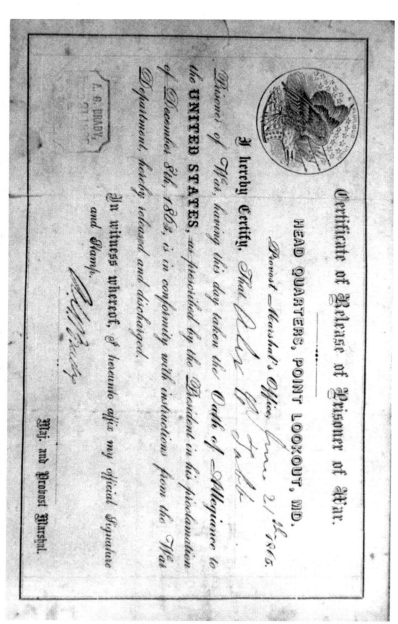

Certificate of Release from Prison for Alex C. Tabb after Civil War

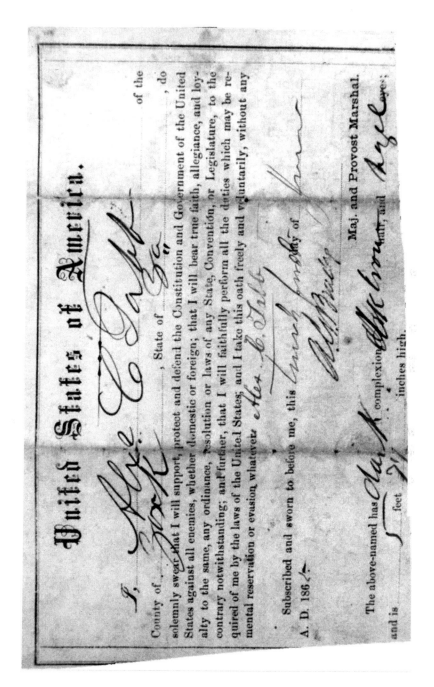

Loyalty oath signed by Alex C. Tabb

Post Office

Postmaster General

To all to w

Whereas, On the ___ 21st day of ___

Postmaster at ___ Tabb ___, in th

whereas she did on the ___ 25th day of ___

as required by law:

Now know ye, That confiding in the i

I do commission her a Postmaster, authoriz

aforesaid, according to the laws of the United

the said Office of Postmaster, with all the pow

of the Postmaster General of the United S

In testimony whereof I have

this ___ graffite

ninety-four

*Certification of Mary
O. Tabb, first Post
Mistress of Tabb Post
Office, Virginia.
Photograph by
Leonard Schwartz*

Mary Octavia Smith Tabb's tombstone, in a cemetery near her Virginia home. The portion at the bottom of the stone says, "She was beloved by everyone that knew her. She knew her duty and did it well."

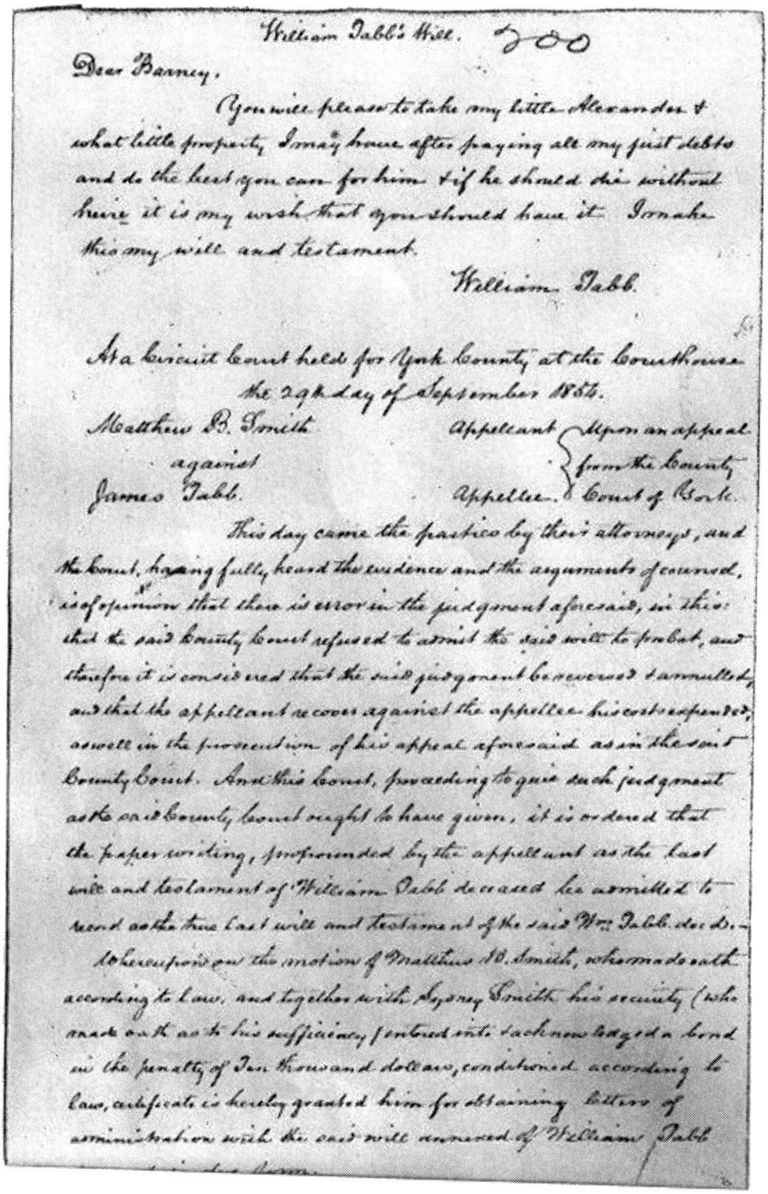

William Tabb's Will. 200

Dear Barney,

You will please to take my little Alexander & what little property I may have after paying all my just debts and do the best you can for him & if he should die without heirs it is my wish that you should have it. I make this my will and testament.

William Tabb.

At a Circuit Court held for York County at the Courthouse the 29th day of September 1854.

Matthew B. Smith Appellant } Upon an appeal
against } from the County
James Tabb. Appellee } Court of York.

This day came the parties by their attorneys, and the Court, having fully heard the evidence and the arguments of counsel, is of opinion that there is error in the judgment aforesaid, in this: that the said County Court refused to admit the said will to probat, and therefore it is considered that the said judgment be reversed & annulled, and that the appellant recover against the appellee his costs expended, as well in the prosecution of his appeal aforesaid as in the said County Court. And this Court, proceeding to give such judgment as the said County Court ought to have given, it is ordered that the paper writing, propounded by the appellant as the last will and testament of William Tabb deceased be admitted to record as the true last will and testament of the said Wm. Tabb decd.

Whereupon on the motion of Matthew B. Smith, who made oath according to law, and together with Sydney Smith his security (who made oath as to his sufficiency) entered into & acknowledged a bond in the penalty of Ten thousand dollars, conditioned according to law, certificate is hereby granted him for obtaining letters of administration with the said will annexed of William Tabb

William Tabb's will. Note the beautiful handwriting.

NOTES

ADDENDUM

The following subjects may be studied in Tavey's diary and elsewhere for a larger view of life in America in the last half of the nineteenth century.

DOMESTIC LIFE
Home (House / Layout / Furnishings / Construction / Etc.)
Food (Diet / Gardening / Fishing / Hunting / Preparation / Utensils / Preparation / Etc.)
Household help (Yes / No / Maybe / Husband, Wife, Children / Servants / Etc.)
Children (Childcare / Education / Entertainment / Clothing / Etc.)
Domestic Skills (Sewing: Clothing – Men, Women, Children / Household / Etc.; Needle work: Crocheting / Embroidering / Tatting / Quilting / Etc.; Cooking and Baking: Food / Diet / Meals / Etc.); Care-giving (Medicine / Home remedies / Doctors / Etc.)

SOCIAL LIFE
Hospitality (Visiting / Dining / Picnics / Parties / Etc.); Games (Charades / Cards / Etc.)

RELIGIOUS LIFE
Churches (Locations / Denominations / Sermons / Socializing / Etc.); Spirituality

COMMUNICATION
Family and Friends (Visiting / Relating news / Writing letters / Etc.); Newspapers

EDUCATION
Schools or Schooling / Materials / Etc.

TRANSPORTATION
Walking / Animals / Wagons / Carts / Etc.

Billie Rose Paxton Einselen

CPSIA information can be obtained at www.ICGtesting.com
Printed in the USA
BVOW041904180612

293022BV00003B/67/P